GREEN GUNNERS

GREEN GUNNERS

Arsenal's Irish

STEPHEN McGARRIGLE

MAINSTREAM
PUBLISHING

EDINBURGH AND LONDON

First published in Great Britain 1991 by
MAINSTREAM PUBLISHING COMPANY
(EDINBURGH) LTD
7 Albany Street
Edinburgh EH1 3UG

ISBN 1 85158 442 0

A catalogue record for this book is available from the British Library

Phototypeset in 11/13pt Garamond by Intype, London
Printed in Great Britain by Courier International, East Kilbride

To my parents Patsy and Susanna

CONTENTS

ACKNOWLEDGMENTS

The author would like to thank the following for the use of their material:

Peter Carbery of the *Irish Post* and David Burke of the *Irish In Britain News* who have made significant contributions of both photographs and interviews; Bill Smith, for his photographs; Fred Ollier whose research for his own book, *Arsenal: A Complete Record* has saved me a lot of leg work; Kevin Connolly MA, author and compiler of Arsenal's official match-day magazine; Eric White, Graham Haynes, Ian Westbrook, Rob Jex, *100 Years of Brentford*; Sean Ryan and Stephen Burke, *The Book of Irish Goalscorers*; Tony Thwaites, *From Sandhall to the Shay*; Dennis Turner and Alex White, *Fulham: A Complete Record*; Doug Lamming, *Who's Who of Liverpool FC 1892–1989*; Ron Atkinson, *United to Win*; Duncan Bond, *Shoot* Magazine.

I am also very grateful to the following for their valuable leads, advice, photographs and patience, and without whose contributions this volume would not have been possible. No doubt they will recognise their contributions in the course of the book:

Terry Neill, Bill Darby, Noel Kivlehan, Seamus McGarrigle, John Dillon, Mariead O'Leocha, Joe Haverty, Bill Smith, Nigel Bishop (Brighton & Hove Albion FC), Denis Clarebrough (Sheffield United FC), Rev. Nigel Sands MA (Crystal Palace FC), Wade Martin (Stoke City FC), Frank Broughton (Hull City FC), Eric White (Brentford FC), Christopher White (Glasgow Celtic FC), M. McKnight (Distillery FC), Robin Marwick (Albion Rovers

FC), Joanna Pool (Leicester City FC), Tony Mundell (Reading FC), David Downs (Reading FC), Yvonne Haines (Fulham FC), Mike Davage (Norwich City FC), J. Greenwood (Everton FC), Peter Cullen (Bury FC), Sid Woodhead and Ron Briggs (Grimsby Town FC), B. Ludge (Bristol City FC), Tony Thwaites (Halifax Town FC), Mrs A. Pettifor (Halifax Town FC), P. A. Weld (Portsmouth FC), Barry Fox (Southampton FC), Dee Elwood (Colchester United FC), Tony Geerts (Bright & Hove Albion FC), James Farry and Peter Donald (Scottish Football League), Malcolm Brodie and Derek McAnneny (*Belfast Telegraph*), Tommy Dunne, Tony Matthews, Peter Woods, Seamus Breslin, Derek Penfold, Marie McCartney and Demelza Jane Flanders.

Last but not least, I would like to convey my most heartfelt thanks to the people who have been most closely involved in the putting together of this book. They are Fiona Dickson, who spent many hours typing the manuscript, Brian Doherty, who edited the original text, and Bill Coffey, whose guidance and advice over the years has proved invaluable.

FOREWORD

The history of Arsenal Football Club is a long and illustrious one, studded with great achievements and displaying a consistency unmatched in the world of football.

For many who have been a part of that history, the true significance of their association with the club is never fully realised until after their departure. Then, and only then, do many understand the expression 'once an Arsenal man – always an Arsenal man'.

This book is a record of the part that the Irish have played in the great history of the Gunners.

It is a welcome tribute not only to the players, but also to those 'unsung heroes' of the game of football – the scouts. These men deserve a place of honour for their unstinting loyalty in maintaining Arsenal's place at the top. During our time as players and managers, we enjoyed a higher profile and the plaudits of the public, but we should never forget the men whose keen eye and good judgment first gave us the opportunity to play.

I am, and always will be, proud of the part I was fortunate enough to play in the history of The Arsenal. I have no doubt that every man whose name figures in this exceptional history feels exactly the same.

Terry Neill

INTRODUCTION

Woolwich Arsenal was first elected to the Football League in 1893. Four years later, in May 1897, Belfast-born Patrick Farrell became the first Irishman to join the club. From that time on, right up to the present day, the trend of acquiring the cream of Irish soccer talent has been central to the youth policy of Arsenal FC. In return, Ireland has obliged by providing the Gunners with no fewer than 36 players, at least 25 of whom achieved international recognition whilst at Arsenal. Every decade has thrown up its Irish gems for Arsenal. In the 1900s, Tommy Shanks' goals shot Arsenal into Division One for the first time; in the 1930s the Gunners acquired the services of one of Ireland's most talented soccer sons in the shape of Jimmy Dunne; the 1960s saw Magill and McCullough, the second of Arsenal's trio of all-Irish full-back partnerships to wear the red and white strip with some distinction, as did manager-to-be Terry Neill. The 1970s, the most memorable decade of them all, gave us among others, Jennings, Rice, Nelson, Brady, Stapleton and the indefatigable O'Leary.

This book is intended as a tribute to those players, and all those other Green Gunners – players, managers and scouts alike – whose names may not trip off the tongue quite so easily, but who have made varying contributions to the development of Arsenal FC into the most powerful soccer force in the land, and who together make up Arsenal's Irish Connection.

TWENTY FACTS ABOUT ARSENAL'S IRISH STARS

* Belfast-born Patrick Farrell became the first known 'Green Gunner' when he joined Arsenal from Celtic in May 1897.
* Four months later, on 1 September, he became the first Irishman to score a league goal for Arsenal when he found the target on his debut against Grimsby Town.
* Other Irishmen to mark their debut with a goal include David Hannah, Maurice Connor, James Hopkins, Terry Neill and Niall Quinn.
* Irishmen who have had the honour of captaining the Gunners include Terry Neill, Pat Rice, Terry Mancini and David O'Leary.
* Despite the fact that a large proportion of Arsenal's Irish have been defenders, Green Gunners overall have contributed more than 350 goals to the Arsenal cause.
* Frank Stapleton, with 108 goals in major competitions, is Arsenal's top Irish goalscorer.
* Stapleton also holds the Arsenal record for goals scored in the League Cup with 14 successful strikes to his credit.
* When he scored in the 1983 FA Cup final for Manchester United against Brighton, Stapleton became the first player to score for different clubs in two Wembley FA Cup finals, having previously scored for Arsenal against Manchester United in the 1979 showdown.
* That epic 1979 final against United is the last time Arsenal

have won the FA Cup, and the captain on the day was Irish international defender, Pat Rice.

* He was accompanied in the Arsenal team that day by five other Irish international stars, and the team manager was ex-Arsenal and N. Ireland player Terry Neill.

* Rice holds the Arsenal record for appearances in the FA Cup and European competitions, with 67 and 27 respectively.

* He is also the only player to appear in all five of Arsenal's FA Cup finals in the '70s and '80s.

* David O'Leary, with 673 appearances at the end of 1990–91, holds the Arsenal record for appearances in first class matches.

* O'Leary is also the player who has won most Irish international caps whilst at Highbury, with 54 to date, and only ex-England international Kenny Sansom (77) stands ahead of him as the most capped Gunner of all time.

* Overall 25 Irish players have been capped at full level whilst on Arsenal's books, and to date they have accumulated 383 caps among them.

* Pat Rice won all of his 49 N. Ireland caps as an Arsenal player.

* David O'Leary, when he made his debut against Burnley in August 1975 at the age of 17 years 3 months, became the youngest Irishman ever to appear for the Gunners.

* When Pat Jennings lined up against Sheffield Wednesday in November 1984 he became, at 39 years and 116 days, the oldest player ever to appear in an Arsenal shirt.

* When he lined up for Arsenal to face West Bromwich Albion at the Hawthorns, February 1983, Jennings became the first player to appear in 1,000 first-class matches.

* No fewer than five of Arsenal's Irish acquisitions – Billy Dickson, Jim Harvey, Jack McClelland, Joshua Sloan and Peter Tilley – were born in the Co. Armagh town of Lurgan.

A–Z OF ARSENAL'S IRISH PLAYERS

Kwame Ampadu (photo: Irish Post)

KWAME AMPADU

Born: Bradford, 20 December 1970
Signed for Arsenal: July 1988
League Debut: v Derby County (A) March 1990

It may seem somewhat strange that a book subtitled *Arsenal's Irish* should begin by describing the embryonic career of a player with a name like Kwame Ampadu. Be that as it may, Kwame's brace of substitute league appearances for the Gunners in 1989–90, coupled with his Republic of Ireland Youth and Under–21 caps, earns him his rightful place in this volume.

Although born in Bradford, Kwame was brought up in Dublin and qualifies to play for Ireland via the parentage rule. He played his junior football in Dublin with Sherrards United and Belvedere, before signing for Arsenal in 1988. He made rapid progress through Arsenal's junior sides and soon became a regular in the reserves, helping the Highbury second string to the Football Combination Championship in 1989–90. Kwame made his league debut as a substitute for Paul Davis in the 3–1 victory over Derby County at the Baseball Ground in March 1990. He was on the bench again for the next game, against Everton at Highbury; on this occasion he replaced Kevin Richardson, and once again the Gunners were victorious, overcoming the Merseysiders by a single goal.

During 1990–91 Kwame was farmed out on loan on two occasions, the second period culminating in his permanent transfer to West Bromwich Albion. Initially he spent two months with Second Division Plymouth Argyle who used him as a striker whereas Arsenal, because of an abundance of forwards at Highbury, had preferred to play him wide on the left. Kwame's second loan period began in March 1991 when he joined W.B.A. for a ten week period. During that time he displayed enough potential to persuade Albion manager Bobby Gould to pay the Gunners £50,000 in May to keep Kwame at the Hawthorns on a permanent basis.

A skilful player who combines deft touches with long accurate passes, the only question mark against Kwame is his physical prowess. However, his spell at Home Park combined with a punishing weight training programme will no doubt eventually turn out the finished product, and no doubt he will soon be playing a major part in Albion's drive to regain the Second Division status they lost last season.

LIAM BRADY

Born: Dublin, 13 February 1956
Signed for Arsenal: June 1971
League Debut: v Birmingham City (H) October 1973

Of all the Irish internationals who starred for Arsenal in the 1970s and appeared in all of the club's major cup finals at the close of that decade, Liam 'Chippy' Brady was undoubtedly the outstanding talent. The career of this diminutive midfield genius might never have got off the ground, however, had it not been for the persistence of the Arsenal coaching staff in their efforts to secure his services.

The Liam Brady story began in his home city of Dublin. As the seventh child in a family which had already produced two professional footballers (his brothers Ray and Pat had appeared for Millwall and QPR respectively in the '50s and '60s) it was no great surprise when the youngest Brady became an Irish School-boy international whilst playing with St Kevin's Boys Club in Dublin. It soon became apparent that this particular Brady was something special, and that a bigger stage was inevitable for the talents of the supremely gifted youngster. In 1969 he arrived in north London to become the latest addition to Arsenal's junior playing staff. However, it was not all plain sailing for the young Brady. In later years he was to find out how tough life is at the top, but in those early days he learnt just how difficult it could be at the bottom. Consequently, when he returned to Ireland the following Christmas, Chippy was adamant that he would not return to London. So began five weeks of constant persuasion by Highbury's backroom boys in an effort to get their protégé to return to the fold. Happily, for football lovers around the world, he was won over and in June 1971 Liam Brady became an apprentice Gunner.

Liam developed through the junior teams at Highbury, and in October 1973 he was blooded in the first team, coming on as a substitute for Jeff Blockley in the 1–0 victory over Birmingham

City. For the remainder of that season Brady was in and out of the side, but by 1974–75 he had claimed a regular first team place. When his Republic of Ireland colleagues Frank Stapleton and David O'Leary broke on to the Arsenal scene in 1975–76, Liam was a permanent fixture in the team. It was that combination of Brady and Stapleton which proved so invaluable to Arsenal in the late 1970s. The two Dubliners struck up an understanding which was almost telepathic. Stapleton adequately summed it up when he said of his friend and colleague: 'Liam Brady was the best player I ever played with. He stands out in my mind. I just recall the goals that I scored and the percentage of those goals which he created – there is no other midfielder who comes near him.' Indeed, not many people would argue that as a passer of the ball Brady had few, if any, peers and his dynamic left foot became legendary throughout the football world. His flawless distribution of the ball, allied to a power-packed shot, struck fear into the heart of countless defences.

In May 1978 Brady appeared in his first major final for Arsenal. Unfortunately, not fully fit, he suffered the double heartache of being substituted and seeing his team go down by a single goal to Ipswich Town. He did not have long to wait to make amends, however. The following year the Gunners were back at Wembley to face Manchester United in one of the most thrilling FA Cup finals ever. Brady redeemed himself fully. The master craftsman called upon all of his class, experience, confidence and ability to dictate the pace of the game and became the architect of Arsenal's dramatic last minute victory. The Gunners had threatened to throw away the chance of a victory after conceding a two-goal cushion. With minutes remaining and the sides level at 2–2 a flash of absolute brilliance from Brady set up Alan Sunderland for the winning goal.

In May 1980 the famous twin towers of Wembley beckoned Brady once more. With six fellow Irishmen in the Arsenal line-up – Pat Jennings, Pat Rice, Sammy Nelson, David O'Leary, Frank Stapleton and John Devine – it could almost have been described as an All-Ireland select versus West Ham United. Regrettably, the Irish Gunners could not overcome the Eastenders

Liam Brady (photo: Irish Post)

and for the second time in three years Arsenal had lost an FA Cup final by the narrowest of margins. Just four days after that third successive Cup final appearance, Arsenal were to suffer further disappointment, losing in the European Winners' Cup against Valencia in Brussels. The following summer Brady joined Italian giants Juventus for £600,000, despite the fact that Manchester United were prepared to smash the British transfer fee record with a £1.5 million bid. So ended the era of Brady the Gunner, after more than 300 first team games and a goal tally of 59. The man who had been the linchpin of the Arsenal side for seven seasons, had been the club's 'Player of the Year' three times, Republic of Ireland 'Player of the Year' in 1976 and PFA 'Player of the Year' in 1979, was off to take on a new challenge in the ultra-competitive Italian League.

The Italian League had become something of a graveyard for star players from the English League. Players who had shone in the First Division and then gone to Italy seemed to become mediocre players overnight, unable to adjust to the rigid man-to-man marking system so dear to the Italians. But this player was different. Liam led Juventus to their 19th League Championship in his first season and collected another Championship medal the following year before joining Sampdoria in 1982. He made 57 appearances each for Juventus and Sampdoria before transferring to Internazionale in 1984, for whom he played a further 58 games. Seventeen outings with Ascoli (whom he joined for £500,000, bringing his total transfer fees since going to Italy to over £2m) brought the Italian phase of the Chippy Brady Story to an end.

When he finally decided to return to British football in March 1987 it was not to Arsenal, as many had hoped and expected, but to the club which had deprived him of an FA Cup winners' medal in 1980 – West Ham United.

A serious knee injury in his first season with the Hammers threatened to bring his career to an abrupt and premature halt, but the resilience of the man showed through and he played a further two seasons with United, taking his league appearance tally over the 500 mark and picking up several 'Man of the Match' awards along the way. Described by Upton Park supremo Billy Bonds as a 'manager's dream', Chippy ended his illustrious career at club level by coming on as a substitute for the Hammers against Wolves in May 1990 and scoring a last-minute wonder goal. He left two Wolves defenders for dead as he unleashed a brilliant 20-yard drive into the roof of the Wolves net.

Arguably the best player the Republic has ever produced and certainly the most sophisticated player of his generation, Liam Brady became a folk hero in both London and Dublin. An Irish international for 14 years, he captained the Irish Schoolboys, won 11 Youth caps and collected a record 73 full caps (26 of those as an Arsenal player), scored nine goals and wore the captain's armband on 14 occasions. There was genuine and deepfelt regret when

Liam Brady points the way for Ireland (Billy Strickland Photography)

he decided to retire at international level following his 35th minute substitution against West Germany in September 1989. His last game for his country was in his own testimonial against Finland in May 1990, when the people of his home city turned out in their thousands to pay homage to their favourite footballing son.

Liam was one of the game's true gentlemen and masters, and one who never forgot his roots, as demonstrated by his generous £50,000 donation of his testimonial money to the fight against drugs in Dublin. His somewhat premature retirement left a huge void in a game which today is sadly bereft of talented and skilful players. It was these qualities in abundance which set Liam Brady apart from all the rest.

Liam spent less than a year out of the limelight, during which time he became a players' agent. In June 1991, seeing off stiff competition from his former Arsenal and Ireland colleague Frank Stapleton, he was appointed manager of Glasgow Celtic. Brady's vast experience at home and abroad won the day. Thus at the tender age of 35 he takes his first tentative steps in what hopefully will be a managerial career as successful and illustrious as his playing career.

LIAM BRADY'S ARSENAL CAREER RECORD

SEASON	FOOTBALL LEAGUE		F.A. CUP		F.L. CUP		EUROPE		TOTAL	
	Apps.	Goals	Apps.	Goals	Apps.	Goals	Apps.	Goals	Apps.	Goals
1973–74	9(4)	1	(1)						9(5)	1
1974–75	30(2)	3	2(3)		2	1			34(5)	4
1975–76	41(1)	5	1		1				43(1)	5
1976–77	37(1)	5	3		6				46(1)	5
1977–78	39	9	6		7	4			52	13
1978–79	37	13	10	2	1		4	2	52	17
1979–80	34	7	9		6	5	9	2	58	14
TOTAL	227(8)	43	31(4)	2	23	10	13	4	294(12)	59

Substitute Appearances in Brackets

FRED CLARKE

Born: Kilpike, Co. Down, 4 November 1941
Signed for Arsenal: November 1960
League Debut: v Aston Villa (H) March 1962

One of Arsenal's many acquisitions from Irish League club Glenavon, Fred Clarke joined the Highbury playing staff in November 1960 for a £5,000 fee. A competent, constructive full-back, he spent four seasons at Highbury, mostly in the Gunners reserves as understudy to N. Ireland colleagues Eddie Magill and Billy McCullough. Fred made his league debut, replacing McCullough in the left-back slot in the 4–5 defeat at the hands of Aston Villa in March 1962, in what was to be his only appearance of the season. He had to wait for over a year for his next outing, this time standing in for Magill in the right-back berth. The big breakthrough still failed to materialise and Clarke managed just five full appearances all season.

1963–64 was a carbon copy of the previous season, with Clarke managing five appearances in either of the full-back positions depending on which of his fellow Ulstermen was absent. Injuries to Billy McCullough gave Clarke his most sustained run in the first team in 1964–65, and by the close of that season he had made a total of 17 first team appearances – six more than in the previous three seasons combined.

Capped four times by N. Ireland at Under–23 level during his Highbury days, Fred left north London in November 1965 to rejoin Glenavon.

At first sight, Fred Clarke's Highbury days may appear somewhat lean. However, he did enjoy a measure of success in the Gunners reserves, helping them win the Metropolitan League Professional Cup and the Metropolitan League Cup in 1961, the Football Combination and London FA Cups in 1963 and the Sheriff of London Shield in 1965.

FRED CLARKE'S ARSENAL CAREER RECORD

SEASON	FOOTBALL LEAGUE		F.A. CUP		F.L. CUP		EUROPE		TOTAL	
	Apps.	Goals	Apps.	Goals	Apps.	Goals	Apps.	Goals	Apps.	Goals
1961–62	1								1	
1962–63	5								5	
1963–64	5								5	
1964–65	15		2						17	
TOTAL	26		2						28	

MAURICE CONNOR

Born: Lochee, Dundee, July 1877
Signed for Woolwich Arsenal: May 1902
League Debut: (for Arsenal) v Preston N.E. (A) September
1902

One of football's original wandering minstrels, Joseph John Maurice Connor was born in Scotland of Irish parents in 1877.

Described by the Victorian football scribes as a 'graceful, methodical, right-winger or inside left', Connor did not like to settle with one club for too long and when he retired from the game, during World War One, he had played for no fewer than ten different clubs.

Connor learnt his trade with Lochee Welfare School, Dundee Fereday and the Queen's Gordon Highlanders before joining east Belfast side Glentoran in 1897. Less than a year later, in March 1898, he joined English Second Division outfit West Bromwich Albion for whom he made ten appearances before transferring to Second Division Walsall in June 1899. He hit the target 15 times in 52 outings with the Hornets. Connor spent the 1901–02 season with Walsall's Second Division rivals Bristol City and a further 26 appearances plus nine goals were added to his tally during his brief fling with City.

In August 1902 Connor's one-man tour of football clubs took him to Plumstead, the home of Woolwich Arsenal. The Gunners, then in their tenth season of league football, were desperately seeking a player of proven ability who would score the goals which would take them into Division One. The club had been knocking at the door since they joined the league in 1893, never having been out of the top ten and frequently being in the top five teams of the Second Division. Connor, despite his wanderings, seemed to fit the bill perfectly and an ideal start to his Arsenal career seemed to confirm this. He scored one of Arsenal's goals in their 2–2 draw with Preston North End in the opening game of the 1902–03 league campaign. Unfortunately Maurice's early promise was not fulfilled and, after a further 13 league outings he was off again, this time to Brentford. Once again Arsenal, finishing third, just missed out on promotion. The deal which took Connor to Brentford involved another Irishman, Tommy Shanks, making the return journey from Brentford to Arsenal. Wexford-born Shanks turned out to be the saviour Arsenal had been waiting for. Next season, 1903–04, his 24 goals proved enough to take the Gunners into the top division for the first time ever.

In the meantime, Connor was winning acclaim by becoming Brentford's first ever international player, with a cap against Scotland in Glasgow in March 1903. Lining up alongside Shanks, Connor scored one of Ireland's goals in the 2–0 victory, their first win over the Scots. A week later Connor led the Irish attack again, this time against Wales in Belfast. Ireland were once again victorious by the same two-goal margin, thereby winning a share in the Home International Championship title for the first time ever. But even that accolade could not make him settle, and 25 games and five goals later he was on his way again, for a brief sojourn with New Brompton. In October 1903 he moved again to Fulham where he added another cap to the two he won whilst at Brentford and so became the west London club's first international player. He failed to establish himself in Fulham's Southern League side, making just a dozen appearances and scoring one goal. But in the 1903–04 FA Cup campaign, Maurice surpassed himself by grabbing seven goals in eight games with the Cottagers. Connor's next port of call was Second Division Blackpool. He failed to break into Blackpool's first team and returned to Glentoran around 1905. His last known club was Treharms FC whom he joined in 1908.

Maurice Joseph Connor possessed the ideal physical requirements for a winger, standing just 5'7" and weighing in at 11 stone. Although he made over two hundred league appearances he possibly did not achieve his full potential as a winger. This may have been due, in some measure, to his inability to settle at any one club for any length of time. Indeed, the soccer manuals of the day frequently refer to him as an excellent player with an abundance of natural ability. Maurice died in Scotland in August 1934 at the age of 57.

JOHN DEVINE

Born: Dublin, 11 November 1958
Signed for Arsenal: October 1976
League Debut: v Leeds United (A) April 1978

John Devine was first invited to Highbury as a promising young-ster as early as 1973. One of a batch of young hopefuls from Dublin (which also included David O'Leary), he was given just one week to prove that he possessed the qualities necessary to make it as a professional footballer. A year later John returned to Highbury as an apprentice, and in October 1976 signed on as an Arsenal professional.

An attacking right-back of genuine quality, John came to Arsenal at a time when N. Ireland international Pat Rice had a virtual stranglehold on the right-back berth. Rice, one of Arsenal's most consistent performers in the '70s, had missed just a handful of league games since breaking into the first team in 1970. Devine arrived on the scene in 1976 when Rice was in the middle of an unbroken run of 122 league games, and consequently he had his work cut out. However, the newcomer remained unperturbed by the enormity of the task which lay ahead – that of ousting Rice.

Towards the end of 1977–78 an injury brought Pat Rice's amaz-ing sequence of matches to an abrupt halt and gave Devine an opportunity to prove his worth in the first team. John made his debut in Arsenal's 3–1 victory over Leeds United at Elland Road in April, and appeared in two of the remaining three league fixtures that season. With Rice back in the reckoning for the new season, Devine rarely got into the team list and managed just seven outings throughout 1978–79. The following season, Devine shared the right-back position with Rice, adding a further 20 appearances to his league tally. Ironically, although the two Irishmen had been vying for the No. 2 shirt for almost three seasons, when Terry Neill announced the team to face West Ham in the 1980 FA Cup final both players' names appeared on the teamsheet! Rice was at right-back and Devine in the left-back position at the expense of

31

yet another Irishman, Sammy Nelson. In the event, though, it was a forgettable occasion for Devine. He was substituted, and Arsenal lost the tie by a single goal.

The 1980–81 league campaign began with John Devine as the first choice right-back. Not only did he oust Pat Rice from the side but he kept him out – so much so that in November 1980, Pat was sold to Watford. But in many ways Rice's departure, easing the competition for the No. 2 shirt, was Devine's undoing. He relaxed, his application became sloppy and he lost his place, managing just 20 appearances in two seasons. At the close of the 1982–83 season, he was sold to Norwich City where he spent just over three years before embarking on an ill-fated move to Stoke City in November 1985.

Towards the end of 1985–86 he sustained a particularly nasty broken leg following a challenge by Eric Young at Brighton. Although the injury all but ended Devine's career, he remained at the Victoria Ground under contract but never recovered sufficiently to get back into the first team. After Stoke, John joined Norwegian side IK Start with whom he remained for about 18 months before returning to England for a brief period. He then went to India, where he spent seven months guesting for various clubs with a bit of coaching thrown in. Thereafter, John returned to his native Dublin and now plays for Shamrock Rovers.

Nicknamed 'Joker' because of his happy-go-lucky, easy-going attitude, John had a somewhat chequered career, and he never again found his feet after his departure from Arsenal. In six seasons at Highbury, he made over 100 first team appearances and won seven Republic of Ireland caps. He added another five caps during his days at Carrow Road, Norwich.

JOHN DEVINE'S ARSENAL CAREER RECORD

SEASON	FOOTBALL LEAGUE		F.A. CUP		F.L. CUP		EUROPE		TOTAL	
	Apps.	Goals	Apps.	Goals	Apps.	Goals	Apps.	Goals	Apps.	Goals
1977–78	3								3	
1978–79	7						1		8	
1979–80	20		5		3		5		33	
1980–81	38(1)		1		4				43(1)	
1981–82	10(1)				1		2		13(1)	
1982–83	8(1)								8(1)	
TOTAL	86(3)		6		8		8		108(3)	

Substitute Appearances in Brackets

John Devine

BILLY DICKSON

Born: Lurgan, 15 April 1923
Signed for Arsenal: October 1953
League Debut (for Arsenal): v Charlton Athletic (A)
October 1953

A powerful attacking half-back, Billy Dickson began his football career with Notts County, who were then playing in the old Division Three South. He scored two goals in 21 appearances for County in the immediate post-war period, before Chelsea signed him in November 1947. He came to Stamford Bridge in a player-plus-cash exchange deal which took Chelsea's Tommy Lawton to Meadow Lane. Billy spent five seasons at the Bridge making 101 league appearances for his new club and scoring four goals. In 1953 Arsenal manager Tom Whittaker wanted to buy Dickson who was by then regarded as one of the most polished half-backs in the game. In October of that year, Whittaker got his man for a fee of £15,000, and so began Billy Dickson's ill-fated Arsenal career.

Billy's term with the reigning league champions got off to a bright enough start and he made his debut in the same month that he joined the club. The Gunners trounced Charlton Athletic 5–1 – incidentally the only club against whom he was to score during his Arsenal career. He kept his place for the remainder of that 1953–54 season, accumulating 24 first team appearances and missing only a handful of games. But if he had known what fate had in store for him next season, he may have walked out of Highbury there and then. He began 1954–55 wearing the No. 5 shirt, but after only two games into the campaign things began to turn sour. Early in the season he suffered a badly dislocated shoulder, and had barely recovered when a damaged knee put him out of contention once again. To compound matters, a bout of appendicitis at the same time all but put paid to Billy's embryonic Arsenal career.

Chosen to represent N. Ireland on a dozen occasions (three times during his career as a Gunner), Billy joined Mansfield Town in July 1956 where, after 19 appearances, he ended his league career.

BILLY DICKSON'S ARSENAL CAREER RECORD

SEASON	FOOTBALL LEAGUE		F.A. CUP		F.L. CUP		EUROPE		TOTAL	
	Apps.	Goals	Apps.	Goals	Apps.	Goals	Apps.	Goals	Apps.	Goals
1953–54	24	1	2						26	1
1954–55	4								4	
1955–56	1								1	
Total	29	1	2						31	1

DAVID DUNCAN

Born: Co Antrim, 1891
Signed for Woolwich Arsenal: December 1912
League Debut (for Arsenal): v Tottenham H. (H) Dec 1912

Irish-born, Scottish-bred, David Duncan was one of many Scottish based players who were on Arsenal's books at the beginning of the century. As a teenager, David lined up for Scottish junior clubs Glasgow St Anthony and Bellshill Athletic (a club which, incidentally, is still in existence today) before joining Scottish Second Division side Albion Rovers in September 1910. He remained at Cliftonhill for less than a season, making 29 appearances in seven different positions, including 18 at centre-forward which brought a tally of six goals.

In May 1911 he moved south of the border to join Second Division Fulham. Again he stayed just one season, appearing on nine occasions for the Cottagers, before transferring his services to Woolwich Arsenal in November 1912. He made his debut just two days after signing, in the centre-forward position at home against local rivals Tottenham. Spurs ran out 3–0 winners on the day and Davy did not play again until the following January. He managed to get his name on the scoresheet on his second outing, away to Newcastle, but the Magpies' three strikes in reply reduced Davy's first goal for his new club to insignificance. Duncan made just one more league appearance for Arsenal before dropping out of football for a time.

With a total of only five appearances in an Arsenal shirt, it must be said that Davy Duncan's stay at Plumstead was less than satisfactory. It was also true, however, that the club was in deep crisis at the time and there was talk of amalgamation with Fulham. Arsenal used no fewer that 30 players in their 1912–13 campaign and finished with one of the worst playing records in the league, winning just three games all season. They ended with only 18 points from 38 games and were, not surprisingly, relegated to the Second Division. In August 1916 Davy reappeared at Cliftonhill.

This time he spent five years with Rovers, turning in 173 performances before retiring in 1921.

Davy Duncan was hardly one of Arsenal's all-time greats, and it would appear that he was only happy when he was a player with Albion Rovers. During his second spell with the Scottish club, he had lost none of his versatility by all accounts, playing wherever requested with equal composure and consistency. In the latter stages of his career he dropped back to a more defensive role.

JIMMY DUNNE

Born: Dublin, 3 September 1905
Signed for Arsenal: September 1933
League Debut (for Arsenal): v Middlesborough (H)
September 1934

One of the most outstanding players of his generation, Jimmy Dunne is widely acknowledged as the greatest centre-forward Ireland has ever produced. Unfortunately, for Arsenal followers, he will be best remembered as a Sheffield United player.

Like many other Irish soccer stars, the foundations of Dunne's successful career in soccer were laid in his native Ireland as a Gaelic footballer. It was following his release from internment in 1923, after the Irish Civil War, that he changed to Association rules and joined Shamrock Rovers as an outside left. At that stage in Jimmy's career, there was little to indicate that here was a footballing legend in the making. The amazing metamorphosis took place when Rovers switched him to a central striking role where he proved a revelation. Jimmy's rapid transformation and obvious potential did not go unnoticed among the English professional clubs. In 1925 he joined Third Division side New Brighton, where, in his first eight league games, he scored six goals. Less than four months later, he signed to First Division Sheffield United for a £700 fee.

His career at Bramall Lane was nothing less than breathtaking, etching his name indelibly in the history books of that great club. To begin with, United let their new acquisition develop in their reserve side for three years, and when they let him loose on the unsuspecting Sheffield public in 1928, it was obvious that they had found something extra special. Jimmy Dunne combined powerful heading skills with that rare ability to shoot accurately with either foot. This was allied to superb ball control and that instinctive sense of correct positioning which singled him out as the perfect centre-forward.

In the 1929–30 season he scored 36 goals in 39 league games.

Jimmy Dunne in 1930

The following season he averaged a goal a game, finishing top First Division scorer with an incredible 41 goals in 41 matches, a club record which will probably never be surpassed. When he left Bramall Lane in 1933, Dunne had notched up a total of 140 goals in 162 league outings.

In March 1932 legendary Arsenal manager, Herbert Chapman, made the journey north to Yorkshire in an attempt to lure Jimmy to Highbury, but the two clubs failed to negotiate a deal and Chapman returned to London empty-handed. Undeterred by this setback, the Arsenal boss waited patiently for the right opportunity, and in September 1933 he was ready to try again. This time the clubs agreed on a transfer fee of £8,250 (which was an enormous sum of money at the time), and Jimmy Dunne was transformed from a Blade to a Gunner in one fell swoop.

The deal was clinched on the morning of Saturday, 30 September 1934, and that same afternoon Dunne lined up for his new club at Highbury against Middlesborough. Although Jimmy did not get his name on the scoresheet, the Gunners recorded their best win of the season by thrashing the visitors 6–0. Perhaps the 'Boro players, being too busy keeping the new arrival with the big reputation in harness, forgot about the other ten Gunners on the pitch. They, given the extra space, exploited the situation to the full.

Jimmy got his Highbury career off to a relatively good start with nine goals in his first 15 games. Things began to deteriorate after this, however. A round of half a dozen games without a goal and Dunne's position as first choice centre-forward looked tenuous. The arrival on the Arsenal scene of another great shooting star, Ted Drake, in March 1933 compounded the situation and Jimmy's career with Arsenal looked like ending almost before it had begun. Drake took over almost immediately and Dunne did not get another game that season. The pain of being dropped, however, may have been eased by the Championship medal he collected at the end of Arsenal's successful defence of their title. His tally of nine league goals had, without doubt, made a valuable contribution to the club's continuing success. Next season, 1934–35, Jimmy was restricted to just one league outing by the magnificence of Drake (who incidentally scored 42 goals in 41 league games in Arsenal's third successive Championship winning year). Reduced to making only half a dozen appearances the following season, the end of Jimmy's tenure with Arsenal was approaching, and in July 1936 he joined Second Division Southampton for a fee of £1,000. He scored 17 goals in 50 league games for the Saints before returning to Ireland as captain-coach of Shamrock Rovers in November 1937. He led the Hoops to the Irish League Championship that season, retained it the next and crowned those achievements with victory in the FAI Cup in 1940. In 1942 he joined Rover's Dublin rivals, Bohemians, as their coach, where he remained for five years before returning to Milltown and Shamrock Rovers in a similar capacity.

One of only a handful of players to be capped for both N. Ireland and the Republic, Jimmy won seven caps for the former and 15 for the latter. Three of his Republic caps were won during his sojourn with Arsenal. A quiet, modest and unassuming man, Jimmy Dunne was a perfect gentleman both on and off the field of play. His untimely death at the age of 44 in 1949 caused deep, widespread and genuine regret among all who had the pleasure of knowing him, either as a footballer or as a person.

JIMMY DUNNE'S ARSENAL CAREER RECORD

SEASON	FOOTBALL LEAGUE		F.A. CUP		F.L. CUP		EUROPE		TOTAL	
	Apps.	Goals	Apps.	Goals	Apps.	Goals	Apps.	Goals	Apps.	Goals
1933–34	21	9	4	3					25	12
1934–35	1								1	
1935–36	6	1							6	1
TOTAL	28	10	4	3					32	13

PATRICK FARRELL

Born: Belfast, 3 April 1872
Signed for Woolwich Arsenal: May 1897
League Debut: v Grimsby Town (H) September 1897

When Patrick Farrell joined Woolwich Arsenal in May 1897, he became the first in a long and distinguished line of players from Ireland to wear the famous Arsenal shirt. Farrell began his professional career with Glasgow Celtic, where he earned a reputation as an industrious centre-half with great vision and pace. He spent just one season in Scotland before Arsenal, in an effort to bolster their drive for First Division status, lured him south of the border. His transfer caused quite a bit of excitement at the time and the *Woolwich Gazette* of May 1897 was glowing in its praise of the newcomer. It described him thus: 'Without a doubt Farrell is a player of great ability, his cool, thoughtful play being streets in front of any centre-half we have had. He possesses great judgement and tact. Rarely if ever gets bustled and almost invariably effective in his effort to stop progress.'

Patrick made his debut for the Gunners in the first game of the 1897–98 season at home to Grimsby Town. The home team ran out 4–1 winners and the debutant marked the occasion with one of the goals. At the end of the season, Farrell had made a total of 19 league appearances and the Gunners finished fifth, their best position since joining the league in 1893. Surprisingly, though, despite his success with Arsenal, Farrell was transferred to Brighton United during the close season.

He was with the seaside club only two seasons before they folded, whereupon he returned to Ireland to ply his trade with Distillery. In his one season with the Belfast club, Farrell gained international recognition for the first time, winning caps against Scotland and Wales in 1900–01. The following year, however, he was back in England with Brighton's newest club, Brighton and Hove Rangers, a semi-professional outfit formed from the remnants of Brighton United and North End Rangers. Farrell was one of the club's professional players and in 1902–03 he helped Rangers to the championship of Division Two in the Southern League. In the 1903–04 season, Patrick played another four games for Brighton and presumably left at the end of the season, as no other records of him exist in the Football League.

PAUL GORMAN

Born: Dublin, 6 August 1963
Signed for Arsenal: July 1979
League Debut: v Manchester City (A) March 1982

Paul Gorman joined Arsenal as an apprentice in July 1979 and signed professional forms with the club in September 1980. In almost five years at Highbury, he managed just half a dozen first team appearances.

Gorman spent most of his time at Highbury playing in the reserves and junior sides with whom he made over 250 appearances in all competitions and was a member of the Football Combination winning side in 1984. He was given a chance in the first team in 1981–82, in the wake of Liam Brady's departure to Juventus. Two years after he left, Arsenal were still trying desperately and failing miserably to replace him in the midfield pivotal position. Gorman became the latest to try Brady's No. 7 shirt for size when he made his debut in March 1982 in the 0–0 draw with Manchester City at Maine Road. He kept his place for the next three league games but was substituted in the latter two. He had to wait almost two years before he got a second chance to prove his worth. That came in November 1983 when he went on as a substitute for Alan Sunderland in a game against Ipswich. He was in the starting line-up to face Everton the following week in what turned out to be his last senior game in an Arsenal shirt. In June 1984 he joined Birmingham City on a free transfer and made just six first team appearances for the St Andrews club before joining Carlisle United for £10,000 in March 1985.

Gorman spent four and a half years at Carlisle, years which witnessed a steady decline in the fortunes of the Brunton Park club. They were relegated from the Second to the Fourth Division in successive seasons between 1986 and 1988. Gorman made over 200 league appearances for the Cumbrians during this period. In December 1989, following a brief spell on loan to League of

Ireland club Shelbourne, Paul joined Third Division Shrewsbury Town.

A former Schoolboy international, Paul Gorman won over 20 Republic of Ireland Youth caps during his spell at Highbury. He has also been capped by his country at Under-21 level.

Paul Gorman (photo: Bill Smith Photography)

46

DAVID HANNAH

Born: Raffrey, Co. Down, 28 April 1867
Signed for Woolwich Arsenal: October 1897
League Debut (for Arsenal): v Walsall (A) November 1897

The Hannah family left Ireland in the 1870s to begin a new life in the small Scottish town of Renton in the Vale of Leven, and at the tender age of 13 David secured his first employment in the town's dyeworks. Although standing just 5'6" and weighing a little over 11 stones, the young Hannah was soon showing promise in local football. He began as a reserve in the local team and displayed so much innate ability in his role as a jet-heeled winger that in 1889 he was lured across the Scottish border to join First Division Sunderland. David spent five seasons at Roker Park playing on both wings and at inside right. His term with Sunderland was a very productive one, and won him League Championship medals in 1892 and 1893. In November 1894 the pocket dynamo transferred his services to Second Division Liverpool for whom he made 31 appearances, again playing on either wing or at inside right. He also managed a dozen goals along the way, and in 1896 he capped his Anfield career with a Second Division Championship Medal.

Around 1897 Hannah returned to Scotland to ply his trade with Scottish First Division club Dundee. However, his stay at Dens Park was a brief one, and in November of that year he joined Woolwich Arsenal. Less than a fortnight after signing, David lined up for the Gunners in the Second Division fixture away to Walsall. Although the new boy marked his debut with a goal, he couldn't prevent Walsall ending the match 3–2 winners. He continued in the same scoring vein for the remainder of that 1897–98 season, notching up a grand total of 12 goals, including a hat-trick in the home game against Small Heath in March 1898. Those 12 goals confirmed Hannah as joint-leading scorer in the league that season, and this was in spite of the fact that he appeared in only two thirds of all fixtures. He contributed in no small way to Arsenal's final position of fifth, their best since joining the league in 1893.

David's celebrated scoring touch seems to have deserted him in his second season at Arsenal's Manor Ground. In 26 league outings, he found the net on just five occasions, and in April 1899 he played his 50th and final senior game for Arsenal.

DAVID HANNAH'S ARSENAL CAREER RECORD

SEASON	FOOTBALL LEAGUE		F.A. CUP		F.L. CUP		EUROPE		TOTAL	
	Apps.	Goals	Apps.	Goals	Apps.	Goals	Apps.	Goals	Apps.	Goals
1897–98	20	12	3						23	12
1898–99	26	5	1						27	5
TOTAL	46	17	4						50	17

JIM HARVEY

Born: Lurgan, 2 May 1958
Signed for Arsenal: August 1977
League Debut: v Derby C. (A) May 1978

Jimmy Harvey's career as a professional footballer looked bright when, at the close of the 1976–77 Irish League season, he was named 'Young Player of the Year'. Less than three months later, Harvey had signed on the dotted line for Arsenal in a deal which made Glenavon £30,000 richer. However, Jimmy's career in the top flight barely got off the ground and has certainly been dwarfed by later events.

Manager Terry Neill gave Harvey his first taste of league football when he picked him to appear in the final fixture of the 1977–78 season. It turned out to be a baptism of fire for Harvey as the Gunners finished on the wrong side of a 3–0 thrashing at the hands of Derby County. Harvey was again in the line-up for the first game of the following season, a home fixture against Leeds United. The Gunners fared somewhat better on this occasion, sharing the spoils after a 2–2 draw, with Liam Brady scoring both goals for the home side. Jimmy made just one more league appearance for Arsenal, this time as a substitute, before going to Hereford United on loan in the early months of 1980. In March 1980 he joined United permanently on a free transfer. Harvey spent exactly seven years at Edgar Street, playing 276 league games and scoring 39 goals. As well as earning himself a reputation as one of the finest schemers in the lower divisions, he contributed immensely to Hereford's struggle to gain stability in their relatively new environment as a league club.

In March 1987 he left Hereford for Third Division Bristol City, where he remained for just six months, and played in only three league games. Then, following a brief period on loan to Wrexham, he joined Fourth Division Tranmere Rovers for £25,000 in September. As club captain at Prenton Park, he has guided the Merseysiders from Fourth Division obscurity to one of the most formidable sides in the Third. In the past two seasons Harvey has led the Rovers to Wembley on no fewer than four occasions. In both 1989–90 and 1990–91 the Prenton Park club contested both the Division Three play-offs final and the Leyland Daf Trophy final.

They suffered defeat at the hands of Notts County in the 1989–90 play-offs final just eight days after lifting the Leyland Trophy following the 2–1 victory over Bristol Rovers. A virus kept Harvey out of Tranmere's defence of the trophy in 1991 and Rovers went down 2–3 to Birmingham City. Six days later Harvey was named as substitute in the side to face Bolton in the play-offs final. He came on during the second half and helped Rovers to a 1–0 extra-time victory, thus catapulting the club into Division Two after a 52-year exile.

Now aged 33, Jimmy Harvey has accumulated over 400 league appearances and there still seems to be plenty of life left in his old legs. He now looks set to lead Rovers on their return to Division Two, the only division in which the old veteran has never appeared.

JOSEPH HAVERTY

Born: Dublin, 17 February 1936
Signed for Arsenal: July 1954
League Debut: v Everton (A) August 1954

Never able to settle long in one place, Joe Haverty played soccer for eight different clubs in four countries and on two continents. Like so many other Irish stars he learnt his trade in the League of Ireland with Home Farm and latterly St Patrick's Athletic before treading the familiar route to North London and Arsenal. The man in the Highbury hot seat at the time, Tom Whittaker, was not deterred by Joe's slight frame – he stood only 5'3" and weighed just 9st 6lb. He was one of the smallest players ever to wear the famous Arsenal shirt, or any other shirt for that matter. Be that as it may, Joe's cheeky ball skills and nifty footwork on the wing more than made up for any physical shortcomings. One of the most popular figures in the game in the 1950s, he enjoyed nothing more than twisting, turning and skipping past much bigger defenders who must have felt that trying to halt the little man was akin to attempting to pick up mercury with a fork.

Joe got his chance in the first team, just a month after arriving at Highbury, in the 1–0 defeat at Everton in August 1954. His name featured in the starting line-up on five more occasions that first season, a season in which Arsenal used no fewer than thirty players in their league programme. During the next season, 1955–56, Joe followed a similar pattern with eight successive games towards the end of the season. However, the little wing wizard's inclusion in the side coincided with Arsenal's best run of the season. It began with a 1–1 home draw with Manchester United, followed by six straight wins which pulled the club up to a respectable final fifth position in the league. Soon after the beginning of the 1956–57 league campaign, Joe won a regular first team place and missed only three games of the 31 remaining that season. In his next four seasons at Highbury, however, he was plagued by

Joe Haverty in 1959

injury, and seldom got the opportunity for a long unbroken first team run.

Joe left Arsenal in August 1961 to join Blackburn Rovers for a £17,500 fee. The move turned out to be a failure and, shortly afterwards, Joe was on the way back to London to ply his trade with Fourth Division Millwall. He played 68 league games for the Lions, and helped them win the Fourth Division Championship in 1963 before leaving them too. After playing only one match for Glasgow Celtic in December 1964, he joined Bristol Rovers – but left them having made 13 appearances. This was followed by a return to Ireland, where his career had begun over ten years previously. Spending less than two years with Shelbourne, Haverty needed another challenge, and his chosen destination this time was America, the club Chicago Spurs.

Due to various problems, such as his injuries, it is quite likely that Joe Haverty never reached his full potential as a professional footballer. Following Arsenal's decision to part company with him in 1961, he never settled anywhere, probably believing, like most of his contemporaries, that the only stage big enough for his delicate ball skills was the one where he began his Football League career – Highbury. This is borne out by his record: he made a total of 223 league appearances in English football, 115 of those as a Gunner, and scored a total of 35 goals, 25 of which were for Arsenal.

If Joe's career at club level seems like a series of ifs, buts and what-might-have-beens, his international record was one of smooth continuity. Following his Republic of Ireland debut against Holland in May 1956 he became recognised as Ireland's regular outside left. Through all his trials and tribulations at club level, the international selectors never lost faith in the little man's undoubted ability – so much so that he was capped with every club he played with, adding a further 17 caps to the 15 he had won whilst at Highbury.

One other significant figure of Joe Haverty's career merits comment. It was the popularity, respect and admiration which he aroused in both players and fans alike; wherever he travelled, he was a prince among footballers and gentlemen.

JOE HAVERTY'S ARSENAL CAREER RECORD

SEASON	FOOTBALL LEAGUE		F.A. CUP		F.L. CUP		EUROPE		TOTAL	
	Apps.	Goals	Apps.	Goals	Apps.	Goals	Apps.	Goals	Apps.	Goals
1954–55	6		1						7	1
1955–56	8	2							8	2
1956–57	28	8	4	1					32	9
1957–58	15								15	
1958–59	10	3	1						11	3
1959–60	35	8	2						37	8
1960–61	12	4							12	4
TOTAL	114	25	8	1					122	27

COLIN HILL

Born: Hillingdon, 12 November 1963
Signed for Arsenal: August 1981
League Debut: v Norwich C. (A) April 1983

Colin Hill may justifiably be compared to good wine, in that he
seems to improve with age. One of the most underrated players
in the league, he is now back playing First Division football for
the first time in five years. In recent times, Hill has earned quite
a reputation for being something of a utility man – an aspect of
his game which first became apparent when he was a youngster
at Highbury. Hill joined Arsenal as an apprentice in the late '70s
and agreed professional terms with the club in 1981. He broke
into the Gunners first team towards the end of 1982–83, making
his debut in midfield in the defeat by Norwich at Carrow Road
in April. An injury to striker Graham Rix in that same game
opened the door fully for Hill, and he immediately took over
Rix's striking role, appearing in that position for the remaining
six games of the campaign.

Colin began the 1983–84 season as a regular first-teamer, partnering Irish international David O'Leary – though this time at
centre-half. He made 14 appearances in that position at the beginning of the season and finished the same campaign with a run of
16 games at right-back! With the arrival of Tommy Caton and
Viv Anderson at Highbury in 84–85, Hill found himself out of
favour and spent part of the season on loan to Brighton. He
managed just two league appearances that season and in December
1984 he played his last game for the Gunners – at left-back!

When his Arsenal days ended, Hill left not only the club, but
the country too, joining Portuguese side Maritimo in 1986. He
spent just one season with the First Division club and, by all
accounts, was their outstanding player that year. On his return to
Britain in 1987, Colin signed for Fourth Division Colchester. In
two seasons at Layer Road he made 69 league appearances, most
of which were in his favoured central defensive position, but he

Colin Hill in action for N. Ireland v. Poland in 1991
(photo: Belfast Telegraph)

Colin Hill in Sheffield United strip
(photo: courtesy of Denis Clarebrough)

was also once again employed as a dexterous utility player. In July 1989 Hill moved up two divisions when he joined Sheffield United for a fee of £85,000. In his first season at Bramall Lane he made 43 first team appearances, all at right-back, and helped the Blades win promotion to Division One, after a 15-year absence.

A quality player with a good first touch and an accurate distribution of the ball, Colin Hill's undoubted ability seems to have gone unnoticed by the media and international selectors alike – until recently that is. Eligible to represent N. Ireland because of his father's Irish background, Hill was included in the N. Ireland squad for the game against Israel in 1984, but failed to make the final XI. In March 1990, however, at the age of 26, Hill won his first N. Ireland cap and became the first Sheffield United player to be capped under the banner of N. Ireland as opposed to 'Ireland'.

Although in the autumn of his playing days, Colin's career seems to be on the way up. Sheffield United have given him First Division status once more, and N. Ireland have made him an international player, so perhaps he may now get the recognition he deserves, and Arsenal will rue the day they let the raw youngster walk away from Highbury.

James Hopkins (photo: courtesy of Nigel Bishop)

JAMES HOPKINS

Born: Belfast, 12 July 1901
Signed for Woolwich Arsenal: September 1919
League Debut: v West Brom. A. (A) March 1921

James Hopkins served his apprenticeship in his home city, playing with Belfast United and Willofield United, and in September 1919 he crossed the Irish Sea to join Arsenal. A frail teenager, standing 5′ 7″ and weighing just 10 stone, James looked the most unlikely professional footballer. However, his slight frame belied an inner courage and strength more befitting a much bigger man. A soccer scribe of the day described him thus: 'not overburdened with avoirdupois but his cleverness of touch and indefatigable energy are ample compensation for his lack of inches'.

James's fortunes at Highbury were somewhat mixed. He was often troubled by illness and injury which kept him out of the side for long periods at a time. But when he was match-fit and chosen to play he invariably proved how capable he was. He made the first of his 21 league appearances in an Arsenal shirt in a pulsating game against West Bromwich Albion at the Hawthorns in March 1921. Playing in one of the inside forward positions, he marked his debut with a goal in Arsenal's 4–3 victory. He made a further seven league appearances at the end of that 1920–21 season, including an unbroken sequence of six outings – his longest in an Arsenal shirt.

Hopkins made just 11 league appearances in the 1921–22 campaign, scoring 3 goals along the way. In 1922–23, his last season at Highbury, he recorded a 100 per cent scoring record – unfortunately he played in just two games. He scored Arsenal's consolation goal in their 4–1 beating at Burnley and, in his final game in October 1923, his goal earned the Gunners a draw at Newcastle. Three months later, in January 1923, James was transferred to Division Three South side Brighton and Hove Albion. He fared much better at the Goldstone Ground, earning himself a reputation as a prolific goal-scorer. In seven seasons with the Seagulls

James Hopkins wins a cap for Ireland

he made 219 league appearances, finding the net on 74 occasions, and in 1926 he won his only Irish cap when he was chosen for the game against England.

At the close of the 1928–29 season James left Brighton for non-league club Aldershot.

JAMES HOPKINS' ARSENAL CAREER RECORD

SEASON	FOOTBALL LEAGUE		F.A. CUP		F.L. CUP		EUROPE		TOTAL	
	Apps.	Goals	Apps.	Goals	Apps.	Goals	Apps.	Goals	Apps.	Goals
1920–21	8	2							8	2
1921–22	11	3	1						12	3
1922–23	2	2							2	2
TOTAL	21	7	1						22	7

PAT JENNINGS

Born: Newry, 12 June 1945
Signed for Arsenal: June 1977
League Debut (for Arsenal): v Ipswich town (A) August
1977

Pat Jennings, that brilliant custodian of the Arsenal goal for eight seasons in the 1970s and 1980s, was the complete goalkeeper. He stood 6ft tall, with hands reputed to be the biggest in football. He possessed an agility bordering on elasticity that without doubt made him the best goalkeeper in British football (and possibly the world) during that period.

The big man's career, like that of so many other legends, had humble beginnings. He first pulled on his gloves in the Irish league for his home club Newry Town and it was not long before the big guns across the water were alerted. Manchester United sent scouts to watch Jennings in action but they went to the wrong game – a mistake which must now be regarded by United as a blunder of titanic proportions. Meanwhile, Second Division Watford, who had been impressed by what they had seen of the young Jennings in an international Youth tournament in Bognor Regis, moved quickly and signed him in May 1963. After just a year at Watford, in which he made 48 league appearances, the inevitable happened, and the giant gentleman joined Tottenham Hotspur for what now seems like a bargain £27,000. That move really signalled the beginning of Jennings' illustrious career as Britain's most out-standing 'keeper over the next three decades. In twelve years at White Hart Lane, Pat won honours galore both on and off the field of play. The first of those came in 1967 when he collected an FA Cup winners' medal, after Spurs' 2–1 defeat of Chelsea. That was followed by League Cup winners' medals in 1971 and 1973, and two medals in the UEFA Cup – Spurs won it in '72 and were runners-up in '74.

Football writers named him their 'Footballer of the Year' in 1973, and the Professional Footballers Association bestowed the same honour on him in 1976. That same year he was made an MBE in the Queen's Birthday Honours list, and in 1987 was awarded the OBE.

Pat made over 500 appearances for Spurs, surpassing Ted Ditchburn's record of 418 in 1976–77. Then, at the end of that season, the inexplicable happened: in a blunder that must be regarded as being on a par with Manchester United's original slip-up, Pat was sold to next-door neighbours and arch rivals Arsenal for £45,000. Good news for the Gunners, but if Spurs thought that Jennings was finished at 31 years old, they were very much mistaken. Immediately, he took up the position between the Arsenal sticks that had been occupied by Jimmy Rimmer during the previous three seasons. Pat made his league debut in the 1–0 defeat at Ipswich in August 1977, a game in which he had no fewer than five fellow Irishmen playing in front of him. The remarkable level of consistency which brought him so many rewards at Spurs was by no means diminished by his short trip across North London. In his first season at Highbury he was the only Gunner to appear in all 42 league fixtures, as well as taking part in all of Arsenal's 13 games in the two major cup competitions. Unfortunately, after so much promise early on, the club finished the season empty-handed. They were defeated by Liverpool in the semi-final of the League Cup, a disappointment which was compounded a short while later when the club lost to Ipswich in the FA Cup final.

Willing to try again, Pat and his Arsenal colleagues were back at Wembley the following season to take part in one of the most sensational FA Cup finals Wembley has ever staged in the postwar era. With less than five minutes remaining, and Arsenal leading Manchester United 2–0, the players must have been thinking of the after-match celebrations. United, however, had other ideas in mind and with two deadly thrusts from Sammy McIlroy and Gordon McQueen, it was all square. The game looked set for extra time, when Alan Sunderland caught United still celebrating their dramatic comeback and popped up to score the winner in the dying seconds – and Pat collected his first medal with his new club. Twelve months later, in May 1980, Arsenal made the familiar journey up Wembley Way for their third successive Cup final,

Pat Jennings (photo: Irish Post)

only to lose this time by 1–0 to fellow Londoners West Ham United. The same year Jennings picked up a European Cup Winners' Cup runners-up medal after Arsenal lost to Valencia.

By January 1982 Pat had been at Highbury for four and a half seasons, missing only a handful of league games and being consistently present in the club's remarkable three-year cup run. But in that fateful month he suffered an injury when playing against his old club, Spurs, which kept him out of the team for the remainder of that season and for a substantial part of the next. The 1983–84 season saw Pat back as first-choice 'keeper, taking over from Wood, who had deputised in his absence. But in the middle of the following season's campaign he lost his place to the up-and-coming John Lukic who had been blooded in the first team the previous year. Thus, after 380 appearances in the famous red and white strip, the end of an era beckoned . . . but only at club level.

Pat Jennings takes a break from training, 1978 (photo: Irish Post)

Capped at Youth and Under–23 level, Pat Jennings' full international career began with a 3–2 victory over Wales in Swansea in April 1964, the same night as another relatively unknown Irishman who was also to achieve legendary status, George Best, made his international debut. For the next twenty-two years, apart from a brief period in 1970, Pat was N. Ireland's first-choice goalkeeper – a remarkably consistent record by anyone's standards, and one which put paid to the international aspirations of a constant stream of Irish goalkeepers. The hero of N. Ireland's British Championship successes in the early 1980s and their two marvellous World Cup campaigns in 1982 and 1986, Pat went on to collect a total of 119 full caps, winning 42 of them whilst he was guardian of the Highbury goal. Those 119 caps created a new world record for a 'keeper, that particular distinction being previously held by the legendary Italian Dino Zoff. It was all the more remarkable when one considers that most of those games were in the old Home International series, and that throughout his career N. Ireland qualified only twice for major championship finals, thereby seriously limiting Jennings' opportunities to add to his tally.

Completely imperturbable and a credit to both his country and his profession, Pat ended his career on the highest note possible – against the mighty Brazilians in the 1986 World Cup in Mexico. Thereafter he returned to Spurs in a coaching capacity.

PAT JENNINGS' ARSENAL CAREER RECORD

SEASON	FOOTBALL LEAGUE		F.A. CUP		F.L. CUP		EUROPE		TOTAL	
	Apps.	Goals	Apps.	Goals	Apps.	Goals	Apps.	Goals	Apps.	Goals
1977–78	42		6		7				55	
1978–79	39		11		1		6		57	
1979–80	37		11		7		9		64	
1980–81	31		1		2				34	
1981–82	16		1		4		4		25	
1982–83	19		7		4				30	
1983–84	38		1		4				43	
1984–85	15				3				18	
TOTAL	237		38		32		19		326	

NOEL KELLY

Born: Dublin, 28 December 1921
Signed for Arsenal: September 1947
League Debut: v Everton (A) February 1950

Noel Kelly was a clever little inside forward who began his career with Bohemians and Shamrock Rovers in the League of Ireland. He was playing with Belfast club Glentoran when, in September 1947, Arsenal swooped and took him to Highbury for a fee of only £650.

Kelly's time at Highbury was spent almost exclusively in the reserves, where he scored 16 goals in 74 outings. His only respite from reserve team football came when he was chosen for the team to face Everton at Goodison Park in February 1950. However, that game, which Arsenal won 1–0, turned out to be his one and only senior game in an Arsenal shirt. The following week, Kelly was sold to Crystal Palace in what must be regarded as an astute piece of business acumen on the part of the Arsenal management – the fee was £8,000, over twelve times what they had paid for him less than three years before.

Noel spent less than two seasons at Palace, scoring six goals in 42 league appearances before joining Nottingham Forest in August 1951. He fared better with Forest than with his previous two league clubs, managing 11 goals in 48 league outings and winning his only full Irish cap. Noel's last league club was Tranmere Rovers whom he joined in July 1955, playing in 52 matches and scoring six goals. He later became player-manager of the Birkenhead club before dropping out of the league to become player-manager of Ellesmere Port Town in 1957. He was later manager of Holyhead Town.

ANDY KENNEDY

Born: Dublin, 1 September 1897
Signed for Arsenal: November 1922
League Debut (for Arsenal): v Birmingham C. (H) Dec.
1922

As a youngster Andy Kennedy was on the playing staff of Ireland's greatest ever club side, the now defunct Belfast Celtic. He then had a short spell in the Irish League with Celtic's east Belfast rivals, Glentoran, before setting sail for England in 1920 to sign for Crystal Palace. Andy spent about eighteen months with Palace, contributing to their success in lifting the Third Division South Championship title in 1920–21. In August 1922 he transferred his services to Highbury and Arsenal.

After a few months' acclimatisation in the Gunners' reserves, Kennedy was judged ready for First Division football. He made his debut at right-back in the 1–0 home victory over Birmingham City in December 1922. He held onto his place for the remainder of the season, missing just two games and clocking up a total of 24 appearances. Soon after his breakthrough into the first team, Kennedy was joined in the side by fellow Ulsterman Alex Mackie who laid claim to the left-back berth. As a result, the first of Arsenal's many all-Ulster full-back combinations was born. Kennedy made 29 league appearances in his second season, 1923–24, and in 1924–25 he missed just two matches throughout the league programme. However, what on paper might be construed as a steady rise in Andy's fortunes and stability was accompanied by a steady decline in the fortunes of Arsenal Football Club. In 1923–24 they finished 19th in Division One, eight places lower than in the previous season. The situation worsened in 1924–25 when they slipped one more place to an unacceptable 20th.

Amazingly, however, in 1925–26 the Gunners improved by a massive 18 places, finishing second, thanks largely to a record 34 league goals from Jimmy Brain. The Gunners' welcome change of fortune also signalled an unwelcome change in the fortunes of

Andy Kennedy. From that time on, he was finding himself increasingly out of favour, and in the three seasons following 1924–25 he made just 29 league appearances – the same number he had made in his first full season at Highbury!

In January 1928 Andy was transferred to First Division rivals Everton, but not before he had picked up a memento of his stay at Highbury – an FA Cup runners-up medal. He had not appeared in any of the previous rounds of the 1927 Cup competition, but an injury to the first choice left-back, Horace Cope, just before the final showdown with Cardiff City gave Kennedy his day out at Wembley. Unfortunately, the Welshmen spoiled the occasion by running out 1–0 winners on the day. Andy's stay at Goodison lasted just one and a half seasons and produced only a single league outing in 1928–29. In June 1930 he was transferred to the poor relations of Merseyside, Tranmere Rovers, where he ended his playing career. An Irish international on two occasions, in 1923 and 1925, both while still a Gunner, Andy Kennedy died in December 1963, aged 66.

ANDY KENNEDY'S ARSENAL CAREER RECORD

SEASON	FOOTBALL LEAGUE		F.A. CUP		F.L. CUP		EUROPE		TOTAL	
	Apps.	Goals	Apps.	Goals	Apps.	Goals	Apps.	Goals	Apps.	Goals
1922–23	24		2						26	
1923–24	29		1						30	
1924–25	40		3						43	
1925–26	16								16	
1926–27	11		1						12	
1927–28	2								2	
TOTAL	122		7						129	

ALEX MACKIE

Born: Belfast, 23 February 1904
Signed for Arsenal: February 1922
League Debut: v Birmingham City (H) December 1922

John Alexander Mackie joined Arsenal from Belfast junior side Forth River in 1922. He began his career at Highbury at right back in the Gunners' third team. Nonetheless, his progress was so rapid that by December he was ready to join fellow citizen Andy Kennedy in the Gunners' rearguard. Kennedy had made his first team debut, at left-back on 2 December, away to Birmingham City in a game the visitors lost 3–2. The following Saturday, 9 December, presented a swift opportunity for Arsenal to exact revenge when Birmingham visited Highbury for the return fixture. On this occasion the right-back berth was filled by Alex Mackie instead of England international Frank Bradshaw, who was the regular player in this position at the time. Arsenal ran out 1–0 winners this time and the club's first all-Ulster full back pairing was born. They were trailblazers for similar pairings which were to grace the hallowed Highbury turf in later years such as McCullough and Magill in the 1960s and the most famous of them all – Rice and Nelson – in the 1970s.

Alex Mackie's breakthrough on to the first team scene brought Frank Bradshaw's Arsenal career to an abrupt end. Bradshaw never played for the Gunners again and Mackie became the first choice right-back, missing just one league game out of the remaining 23 fixtures of that season. Coincidentally, that missed game, which was against Preston North End, was also the only game that his partner Kennedy missed that season since making his debut in December. In 1923–24 Alex made a further 31 league appearances but could not halt Arsenal's steady drop to the lower reaches of Division One. They finished 19th, their worst position in the division since 1913. 1924–25 told a similar sorry tale, with the Gunners finishing in a disastrous 20th position. Mackie managed just 19 outings that season, absent through a serious leg injury which was followed by indifferent form, and was replaced by Arsenal's utility player of the time, Alf 'Doughy' Baker.

The 1925–26 season, which initially looked like being another battle for First Division survival, actually turned out to be a race for the Championship title between Huddersfield Town and Arsenal! In the event, the Gunners had to settle for second place behind the Terriers who won the Championship for the third year in succession. 1925–26, as well as being the club's most successful year since they were admitted to the Football League in 1893, was also Alex Mackie's best year since arriving at the club in 1922. Once again he started the season as the first choice right-back alongside Kennedy, and by the end of the campaign had accumulated a total of 35 league appearances. Strange as it may seem, however, towards the end of that season, Alex had played his last game in an Arsenal shirt and was transferred to Portsmouth in the summer of 1928. Mackie spent eight seasons at Fratton Park, adding 257 league appearances to the 108 he had collected as a Gunner. He also made two Wembley FA Cup final appearances for Pompey, in 1924 and 1934, finishing on the losing side both times. In March 1936 he was transferred to Division Three South side Northampton Town where he ended his league career.

Within months of joining Arsenal, Alex was selected to play at right-back for N. Ireland against Wales in Belfast. His partner at left-back on the night, also making his international debut, was none other than Andy Kennedy! Amazingly, it was to be another ten years before Mackie was chosen for Ireland again, when, as a Portsmouth player in 1935, he collected a further two caps.

ALEX MACKIE'S ARSENAL CAREER RECORD

SEASON	FOOTBALL LEAGUE		F.A. CUP		F.L. CUP		EUROPE		TOTAL	
	Apps.	Goals	Apps.	Goals	Apps.	Goals	Apps.	Goals	Apps.	Goals
1922–23	23		2						25	
1923–24	31		2						33	
1924–25	19								19	
1925–26	36		6	1					42	1
TOTAL	108		10	1					119	1

EDWARD MAGILL

Born: Carrickfergus, 17 May 1939
Signed for Arsenal: May 1959
League Debut: v Sheffield Wednesday (A) December 1959

The full-back partnership of Eddie Magill and Billy McCullough at Irish League club Portadown was resurrected in north London by Arsenal boss George Swindin in 1958–59. McCullough was signed for £5,000 in September 1958 and was joined by Magill at Highbury just ten months later.

McCullough was already established at left-back when Eddie made his league debut at right-back in December 1959. However, Eddie's introduction to the big time was hardly memorable, since the Gunners lost heavily 5–1, away to Sheffield Wednesday. It was a similar sad story for Arsenal throughout the season. The club finished in 13th place – their worst league position since 1929–30 when they had finished 14th. At the outset of the following season, 1960–61, the established right-back at the club, Leonard Wills, was given the nod over Eddie for the right-back berth. But in December 1960 the Irishman forced his way back into the side. His first game of the season, almost a year to the day since his debut, was against none other than Sheffield Wednesday at Hillsborough, and no doubt thoughts of the previous encounter between the two sides were prominent in the Ulsterman's mind. He needn't have worried, however, as the Gunners snatched a point thanks to a goal from a rising young star who was none other than future Arsenal and N. Ireland stalwart Terry Neill.

By the time the curtain rose on the 1961–62 league season, Magill had made the right-back position his own. He was by then a team regular, with two seasons and 23 league outings under his belt. He was to retain this position for the next three seasons, partnering Billy McCullough throughout in an all-Ulster full-back pairing. It was during this period that Eddie played the best football of his career, and became regarded as one of the finest defenders in the business. Unfortunately, his purple patch at the

71

top was relatively short-lived. The danger signals were pretty obvious when, in April 1964, Billy Wright (who had since taken over from George Swindin in the Highbury hot-seat) paid West Bromwich Albion £42,000 to bring Don Howe – the future Arsenal manager and England coach – to Highbury. Howe had a reputation as a skilful and cultured defender and at £42,000 he wasn't coming to Highbury to play in the reserves. He immediately ousted Magill from the right-back berth, restricting the Irishman to just one league appearance in 1964–65. In March 1965, the inevitable happened and Eddie left Arsenal. His new club was Brighton and Hove Albion, who at that time were playing out their last few months in Division Four before their elevation to Division Three, a rise which would lead them ultimately to the top flight. Eddie made 50 league appearances for the Seagulls, adding to the 116 he had made at Arsenal, before calling it a day in league football. Thereafter he took up the position of coach to Danish side B1909 Odense, and later had a spell as manager of another Danish side, Frederikshavn.

A former N. Ireland Under–23 cap, Eddie Magill collected a total of 26 full caps for his country, 21 of which were won during the time he was playing his club football at Highbury.

EDWARD MAGILL'S ARSENAL CAREER RECORD

SEASON	FOOTBALL LEAGUE		F.A. CUP		F.L. CUP		EUROPE		TOTAL	
	Apps.	Goals	Apps.	Goals	Apps.	Goals	Apps.	Goals	Apps.	Goals
1959–60	17		3						20	
1960–61	6		1						7	
1961–62	21								21	
1962–63	36		3						39	
1963–64	35		4				4		43	
1964–65	1								1	
TOTAL	116		11				4		131	

TERRY MANCINI

Born: Camden Town, London, 4 October 1942
Signed for Arsenal: October 1974
League Debut (for Arsenal): v West Ham. (H) October
1974

As one of the most colourful and popular characters in the game in the '60s and '70s, Terry or 'Henry' Mancini's arrival at Highbury in October 1974 raised more than a few eyebrows in the football world. Terry was already 32 years old when he joined the Gunners, and looked to be nearing the end of a career which, for the most part, had been spent in the lower echelons of the Football League. He began with Watford in 1961 and made 66 Third Division appearances for the Vicarage Road club before jetting off to South African club Port Elizabeth in 1965. Two years later Mancini returned to the Football League joining Orient, another Division Three side. He made 167 appearances for Orient, picking up a Third Division Championship medal in 1970, before signing for Second Division Queens Park Rangers in October 1971. By 1973, Terry was enjoying his first taste of Division One football, after helping Rangers win promotion to the top flight for the first time in their history. In October 1974 Arsenal boss, Bertie Mee, shocked the football world when he paid the west Londoners a reported £20,000 to take Mancini to Highbury.

'Henry', armed with a ready smile and a quick quip, soon established himself as a great favourite with both the Highbury faithful and the players alike. He made his Arsenal debut soon after signing, in the 3–0 victory over West Ham at Highbury. He immediately established himself at centre-half, ousting veteran defender Jeff Blockley from the team. Terry made a further 25 league appearances in that first season and began the 1975–76 campaign alongside 17-year-old newcomer David O'Leary in the heart of the Gunners' defence. Terry's linking up with his Republic of Ireland colleague provided the explanation for Bertie Mee's decision to buy him. Mee believed Mancini's wealth of experience

73

would help O'Leary develop as a player, and although half-way through the season O'Leary forfeited his place to his mentor who took over the No. 5 position, by the beginning of the next season O'Leary was firmly established in the first team. Mancini, his task complete, was back with Orient in Division Two. He made a further 21 league appearances with Orient before joining Aldershot on a free transfer in September 1976. But less than seven months later in April 1977 Aldershot brought Terry's league career to an end when they cancelled his contract.

Typically, before he left Highbury, Terry had written himself firmly into the annals of Arsenal folklore. His second and final season with the club produced a crop of 26 league appearances, equalling the number of matches he had played in the year before. But in his penultimate game he snatched the only goal of his Arsenal career, and what an important one it was. It salvaged both points in Arsenal's relegation dog-fight with Wolves at Highbury in April 1975, thereby condemning Wolves to the drop. It also ensured that Arsenal's 60-year First Division tenure remained unbroken, despite the Gunners losing their three remaining fixtures.

Despite the misgivings of some about Terry Mancini's ability he proved to be a great asset to the club and by 1975 had impressed so much that he was appointed club captain. He did the job he was bought to do and his resolute defensive qualities more than compensated for any limitations he may have had.

Prematurely bald, with a broad cockney accent, Terry Mancini was one of the most unlikely characters ever to wear the green shirt of the Republic of Ireland. He was the son of an Irish mother and an Italian father, and he hailed from a family more renowned for their boxing skills than for their soccer skills, yet he won five international caps, one of them during his time with the Gunners. When he lined up for his first international appearance, against Poland at Dalymount Park in 1974, he covered his bald pate with a wig, then took it off and waved it to the crowd, thereby winning over the Irish footballing public just as he was to win over the north London fans in the years that followed.

TERRY MANCINI'S ARSENAL CAREER RECORD

SEASON	FOOTBALL LEAGUE		F.A. CUP		F.L. CUP		EUROPE		TOTAL	
	Apps.	Goals	Apps.	Goals	Apps.	Goals	Apps.	Goals	Apps.	Goals
1974–75	26		8						34	
1975–76	26	1			2				28	1
TOTAL	52	1	8		2				62	1

JACK McCLELLAND

Born: Lurgan, 19 May 1940
Signed for Arsenal: October 1960
League Debut: v Tottenham H. (A) January 1961

As a schoolboy Jack McClelland had turned out for a Mid-Ulster Boys' representative side as an inside forward. But when he signed for Irish League club Glenavon years later it was as a goalkeeper. The brilliant Welsh international goalkeeper, Jack Kelsey, was Arsenal's regular custodian when McClelland joined the club in October 1960. Apart from Worcestershire cricketer Jim Standen as Kelsey's understudy, Ian McKechnie, Ian Black, Tony Burns and Bob Wilson were also all waiting for an opportunity to lay claim to the No. 1 shirt – thus making competition for the keeper's position at Highbury very difficult indeed.

In 1960–61 McClelland ousted Standen from the position as Kelsey's replacement and in early 1961 managed a run of four successive league outings. As luck would have it, however, Jack was chosen to make his debut in what is traditionally Arsenal's biggest game of the season – away to arch-rivals Spurs. A more intimidating arena for a young, inexperienced 'keeper would be very difficult to find. In the event, Jack had the unenviable task of picking the ball out of his net four times, as Spurs ran out 4–2 winners. Next season was a mirror image of the previous one with Jack making just four league appearances. But in 1962–63 he got his long awaited break. Jack Kelsey suffered a severe back injury playing for Wales which all but ended his career. Initially it was Ian McKechnie who stepped into the firing line but a poor start to the season by him gave McClelland the chance to prove that he was the man for the job. He made a total of 33 league appearances that season and must have felt quite at home with fellow Ulstermen Eddie Magill, Billy McCullough, Terry Neill and another ex-Glenavon man, Fred Clarke, who together made up almost the entire Arsenal defence. Jack began 1963–64 as first choice 'keeper, although after conceding seven goals against

Leicester City in August McKechnie took over once again. It was the arrival from Liverpool of Jim Furnell in November 1963, however, that sounded Jack's death knell; and in December 1964, after 49 appearances in an Arsenal shirt, he joined First Division rivals Fulham.

At Craven Cottage Jack spent much of his time in the reserves. He spent four seasons with the west Londoners, which included a brief period on loan to Lincoln City in early 1969, and made a total of 57 appearances. In May 1969 Jack was given a free transfer by Fulham. He joined non-League side Barnet, winning an FA Trophy runners-up medal with the north London side following their Wembley defeat by Stafford Rangers in 1972.

A competent, no frills goal-minder, Jack was first chosen to play for Northern Ireland in October 1960, the same month that he became an Arsenal player. He won a further four caps during his Highbury days, adding one more after he had left Highbury for Craven Cottage. Following a short cancer-related illness, Jack McClelland died in March 1976, aged just 35.

JACK McCLELLAND'S ARSENAL CAREER RECORD

SEASON	FOOTBALL LEAGUE		F.A. CUP		F.L. CUP		EUROPE		TOTAL	
	Apps.	Goals	Apps.	Goals	Apps.	Goals	Apps.	Goals	Apps.	Goals
1960–61	4								4	
1961–62	4								4	
1962–63	33		3						36	
1963–64	5								5	
TOTAL	46		3						49	

BILLY McCULLOUGH

Born: Woodburn, 27 July 1935
Signed for Arsenal: September 1958
League Debut: v Luton Town (H) December 1958

Billy McCullough was one of many players who cut their teeth in N. Ireland junior football circles before breaking into the big time. Billy graduated from playing part-time with Barn United and the YMCA club in Carrickfergus, through to Irish 'B' Division side Ballyclare Comrades before getting his chance in the Irish League with Portadown in 1957.

McCullough's elevation to the senior ranks that year provided him with the ideal pad from which to launch a professional career. In the summer of 1958 he was chosen to play for the Irish League in a representative game against the Scottish League. An exceptional outing that day caught the eyes of watching scouts from across the water, but it was Arsenal who moved quickest and in September 1958 paid Portadown £5,000 to get their man.

On arriving at Highbury, Bill quickly settled into the reserve team and got his chance in the first team only three months later, on 27 December, against Luton Town at home. That game was played just one day after the Gunners had lost the corresponding fixture 6–3 at Kenilworth Road. But what a difference the newcomer made – Arsenal ran out 1–0 winners at the end of the second encounter. That first season at Highbury ended with Billy getting a run of eight consecutive games in his favoured left-back position and the team finished third in the league – their best position since they last won the Championship in 1952–3. Soon after the commencement of the 1959–60 assault on the League Championship, McCullough became firmly installed as Arsenal's first choice left-back, a position he was to make his own for six and a half seasons. His appearance record in the middle of his Highbury career was quite exceptional: out of the Gunners' 168 league fixtures in those years, Billy McCullough appeared in an amazing 163! The man's level of consistency is further illustrated by the fact that in the same period the right-back position changed hands no fewer than six times. One of those players who partnered Billy in the Arsenal rearguard was his old Portadown team-mate Eddie Magill.

In 1965–66, following Peter Storey's elevation to the senior ranks, Billy lost his place in the team for the first time since 1959, thereby limiting his first team appearances to 17 that season. It was the end of an era for McCullough and in the close season he joined newly promoted Millwall, who were playing Second Division football for the first time in almost twenty years. Unfortunately his disappearance from the scene was as rapid as his rise to prominence. After only 19 league games for the Lions, he dropped out of league football, joining Bedford Town. Thereafter he had stints as a player-manager in Ireland with Cork Celtic and latterly Derry City.

An all too common feature of Irish players earning their keep on the English soccer scene is that, although they may have been demoted to playing reserve team football, they nevertheless continue to be selected at international level. This is due to the limited player resources available to the I.F.A. and/or the F.A.I. Consequently, an Irish player may appear in more internationals in a given season than in domestic fixtures. In Billy McCullough's case the opposite is true. In eight years playing for one of Britain's foremost clubs he was capped only nine times, adding one more as a Millwall player – cold statistics which completely belie his enormous success at club level.

Billy McCullough in 1959

BILLY McCULLOUGH'S ARSENAL CAREER RECORD

SEASON	FOOTBALL LEAGUE		F.A. CUP		F.L. CUP		EUROPE		TOTAL	
	Apps.	Goals	Apps.	Goals	Apps.	Goals	Apps.	Goals	Apps.	Goals
1958–59	10		1						11	
1959–60	33								33	
1960–61	41		1						42	
1961–62	40		2						42	
1962–63	42	3	3						45	3
1963–64	40	1	4				4	1	48	2
1964–65	30								30	
1965–66	17								17	
TOTAL	253	4	11				4	1	268	5

TERRY NEILL

Born: Belfast, 8 May 1942
Signed for Arsenal: December 1959
League Debut: v Sheffield Wednesday (H) December 1960

Terry Neill's association with Arsenal Football Club spanned four decades and saw him rise from the reserves in 1959 to the first XI in 1960. He became club captain in the early 1970s and finally moved into the manager's chair in 1976.

Neill arrived at Highbury as a raw 17-year-old in December 1959 from Irish League club Bangor City, but his progress in the reserves was so rapid that a year later he was elevated to the first team ranks. Arsenal boss George Swindin blooded the promising youngster in the home league fixture against Sheffield Wednesday in December 1960. Playing at wing half, where Swindin preferred him, Terry marked his debut with a goal which earned the Gunners a point in the 1–1 draw. In those early days at Arsenal, Neill operated as a utility player, appearing at either wing or at centre-half. When Billy Wright took over the managerial reins at Highbury in 1962, he was quick to note Neill's no-nonsense yet skilful play in the back four, and by 1964–65 the Belfastman had earned himself a regular place alongside Scottish international Ian Ure in the heart of the Gunners' defence. Around the same time he was appointed team captain – the youngest player in the club's history to hold that privileged position.

One of the old school of centre-halfs who liked to get forward when the occasion presented itself, Terry's powerful physique and whole-hearted endeavour endeared him to the Highbury faithful. It also presented any opponent with a formidable barrier. His purple patch as a regular member of the first team lasted until the end of 1968, a period in which he made over 200 league appearances. Thereafter, however, with several players vying for the half-back positions, pressure for places became very competitive and Neill could no longer be sure of his first team place. A major

Terry Neill (photo: Irish Post)

reshuffle of the team in 1969–70 saw Terry lose out in the battle for centre-half places to Roberts, McLintock and Simpson. He was consequently restricted to only 17 appearances in what turned out to be his last season as an Arsenal player.

Amazingly, although Neill was one of Arsenal's most loyal and long-term servants, his eleven years as a player at the club yielded just one medal – and a loser's one at that. It came after the 1968 League Cup final defeat at the hands of Leeds United. Terry had played in all previous rounds of the competition that year, but on the day of the Wembley showdown he was named as substitute, coming on to replace Jenkins in the second-half. At the close of 1969–70, with over 300 appearances under his belt, Terry Neill left Highbury to join Second Division Hull City as their player-manager. Between 1970 and 1973 he made 103 league appearances for the Tigers before calling it a day as a player in order to channel all his energies into the management side of the game. In 1974 he was appointed manager of Arsenal's deadly rivals Spurs before returning to Highbury in 1976 to become the youngest ever manager in the great club's long and illustrious history.

An Ulsterman through and through, Terry Neill represented N. Ireland at Schoolboy, Youth and Under–23 levels before winning his first full cap against Italy in Bologna in 1961. For the next twelve years he was a fixture in the N. Ireland set-up, going on to become captain of the side. He won a total of 59 full caps, 44 of those during his Highbury days. Following his transfer to Hull he was chosen to play for his country a further 15 times – a tally that makes him the Boothferry Park club's most capped international player. A former chairman of the Professional Footballers' Association, Neill was once described as the busiest man in football, an apt description since, apart from this role in the late 1960s, he was also, around that same time, player-manager of Hull and player-captain-manager of N. Ireland.

TERRY NEILL'S ARSENAL CAREER RECORD

SEASON	FOOTBALL LEAGUE		F.A. CUP		F.L. CUP		EUROPE		TOTAL	
	Apps.	Goals	Apps.	Goals	Apps.	Goals	Apps.	Goals	Apps.	Goals
1960–61	14	1	1						15	1
1961–62	20								20	
1962–63	17								17	
1963–64	11	1							11	1
1964–65	29	1							29	1
1965–66	39		1						40	
1966–67	34		4		3				41	
1967–68	38	2	4(1)		7(1)	1			49(2)	3
1968–69	21(1)	2			4	1			25(1)	3
1969–70	17	1	2		1		5		25	1
TOTAL	240(1)	8	12(1)		15(1)	2	5		272(3)	10

Substitute Appearances in Brackets

Sammy Nelson in action for N. Ireland v West Germany, April 1977
(photo: Belfast Telegraph)

SAMMY NELSON

Born: Belfast, 1 April 1949
Signed for Arsenal: April 1966
League Debut: v Ipswich Town (H) October 1969

Northern Ireland Schoolboy international Sammy Nelson joined the Highbury playing staff as a 17-year-old in 1966. In fifteen seasons with the club, the quiet, unassuming Belfastman won widespread respect as a classy, stylish left-back, despite the fact that he had joined the club as a winger. It was in that outside-left position that he picked up the first of the many medals he was to win as an Arsenal player; this was a result of the young Gunners' 6–2 aggregate victory over Sunderland in the 1967 FA Youth Cup final.

Towards the end of 1968–69 Nelson converted to left-back, the position in which he made his league debut in the 0–0 draw with Ipswich in October 1969. That first outing only came about due to an injury to the regular left-back, England international Bob McNab. It set the pattern for the next six years – when McNab was out, injured or otherwise, Nelson got in. Consequently, Sammy's appearances were severely limited – to such an extent, in fact, that at the outset he was winning more international caps for Northern Ireland than first team outings for the Gunners.

Meanwhile, he quietly plodded along in the reserves waiting and hoping patiently for the big breakthrough. He may have been comforted during this difficult time by the fact that Arsenal received many generous offers from other top clubs anxious to use his services to the full only to be told that the player's long-term future lay at Highbury. By the end of 1973–74, after seven seasons with the club, Sammy had made just 50 first team league appearances. But the following year the long-awaited break-through materialised. Sammy started a season at Highbury in the first XI for the first time since his arrival as a starry-eyed teenager in 1966. After playing second fiddle to Bob McNab for so long, the tables were turned and Sammy Nelson came of age, linking

Sammy Nelson (photo: Irish Post)

up with fellow Northern Ireland international Pat Rice to form the first-choice full-back partnership at Highbury. At the close of the campaign, McNab was given a free transfer and subsequently joined Wolves. This left the way clear for Nelson to display his considerable, but under-utilised, talents in the most appropriate arena: the Arsenal first team.

It was that rearguard of Rice and Nelson which served both club and country so loyally and so consistently from the mid- to the late-1970s and which formed the backbone of Arsenal's amazing three-year Cup run at the end of that decade. Sammy was one of no less than half a dozen Irish internationals who appeared in all four of the Gunners' major cup finals during that period. He picked up FA Cup runners-up medals after the 1–0 defeat by Ipswich Town in 1978 and, after coming on as a substitute for fellow countryman John Devine, in the 1–0 defeat by West Ham in 1980.

Sandwiched between those FA Cup disappointments was the epic 1979 showdown against Manchester United in which the Gunners overcame the Red Devils in the dying minutes after surrendering a two-goal lead. In May 1980, for the fourth time in two years, Sammy once again lined up alongside his fellow countrymen, Jennings, Rice, O'Leary, Brady and Stapleton for a major final. The venue: Brussels; the occasion: the European Cup Winners' Cup final against Spanish Cup holders Valencia. But once again that by now all too familiar feeling of so near yet so far away was prominent as the Gunners lost the tie in the most cruel fashion of all – going down 4–5 on penalties after a scoreless match.

At the close of 1979–80 Sammy Nelson had accumulated over 300 appearances in an Arsenal shirt, but at the ripe old age of 31 his days at Highbury were numbered. His final match in the famous red and white strip came in the last game of the 1980–81 season (his only one of that season). It had more to do with nostalgia than football when he came on as a substitute for Brian Talbot in the 2–0 home victory over Aston Villa.

In September 1981 Sammy left Highbury to join Brighton and Hove Albion, where he played for a further two seasons before moving behind the scenes at the Goldstone Ground in a coaching capacity until 1984. He became the inspiration behind the little south-coast side's first ever Wembley appearance in 1983. But yet again, for the third time in his career, Nelson had to be content with the runners-up positon in an FA Cup final. Following an inspiring 2–2 draw in the final against Manchester United, the Seagulls were overrun in the replay by their more illustrious opponents and finished the game on the wrong side of a 4–0 thrashing.

Although not as extrovert as Pat Rice, the two Belfastmen provided a very formidable defensive wall. An exciting, adventurous, overlapping full-back, Sammy scaled the heights at international level as well as at club level; an Under–23 international cap was added to his Schoolboy collection even before he had made his league debut. He went on to win 48 full caps as an Arsenal player and was chosen to play for his country a further four times as a Brighton player.

SAMMY NELSON'S ARSENAL CAREER RECORD

SEASON	FOOTBALL LEAGUE		F.A. CUP		F.L. CUP		EUROPE		TOTAL	
	Apps.	Goals	Apps.	Goals	Apps.	Goals	Apps.	Goals	Apps.	Goals
1969–70	4		1				1(1)		6(1)	
1970–71	2(2)				1		0(1)		3(3)	
1971–72	24	1	6		3		5		38	1
1972–73	2(4)		0(1)		1				3(5)	
1973–74	18(1)	1							18(1)	1
1974–75	19(1)				1				20(1)	
1975–76	36		1		2				39	
1976–77	31(1)	3	3		5				39(1)	3
1977–78	41	1	6		7				54	1
1978–79	33	2	10		1		6		50	2
1979–80	35	2	6(1)	1	6	1	7		54(1)	4
1980–81	0(1)								0(1)	
TOTAL	245(10)	10	33(2)	1	27	1	19(2)		324(14)	12

Substitute Appearances in Brackets

KEVIN O'FLANAGAN

Born: Dublin, 10 June 1919
Signed for Arsenal: August 1945
League Debut: v Blackburn Rovers (A) September 1946

A supreme all-rounder, Kevin O'Flanagan was one of that rare breed of men who excel in everything they do. Not only did he line up for Arsenal in the post-war years, but he also played rugby at the highest level, and won the Irish long-jump Championship on four occasions between 1938 and 1943. He was the Irish sprint champion in 1941, a scratch golfer, and an accomplished grass court tennis player.

As a young medical student at University College, Dublin in the late '30s and early '40s, Kevin turned out for Bohemians in the League of Ireland, captaining the side to victory in the 1945 Irish Cup. On completion of his studies in the same year, Dr O'Flanagan took up a medical post in Ruislip, Middlesex. Once in England, O'Flanagan wasted no time in involving himself in extracurricular activities, and in October 1945 made his first Arsenal appearance against Charlton Athletic. Arsenal, then playing out their last wartime season in the Football League South, lost the game 6–2. It was, however, a bitter-sweet experience for the Irish newcomer in that he marked the occasion with one of the Gunners' consolation goals.

At the conclusion of that first season, Kevin had made a total of 18 appearances in both outside right and centre-forward positions and, with an impressive haul of 11 goals, was the club's highest scorer. In the meantime, this marvellous medicine man, not content with his success with the round ball, was displaying his skills with the oval version as a wing threequarter for London-Irish and, in 1948, was capped playing rugby for Ireland against Australia.

When hostilities ceased in 1945, and normal league football resumed, O'Flanagan signed as an amateur at Highbury taking his league bow in the 1–3 home defeat at the hands of Blackburn

Rovers in September 1945. That first league outing was preceded by a brace of appearances in the two-legged FA Cup first round in January of that year, which the Highbury club lost 6–1 on aggregate to fellow Londoners West Ham.

O'Flanagan played a total of 14 league games for the Gunners in that 1946–47 season and scored three goals. In one of those games, versus Stoke City on 19 October, he lined up alongside Albert Gudmundsonn and Bernard Joy who were also amateurs, making up the greatest number of non-professionals to appear in a league side since normal football had resumed in 1946. O'Flanagan marked the event with the winning goal in Arsenal's 1–0 victory.

Unfortunately, his medical commitments curtailed his availability for the club and, after starring for Barnet and Casuals, he signed for Second Division Brentford in 1949. He appeared for the Bees half a dozen times before an ankle injury forced him into early retirement.

An Amateur international in his student days, Kevin progressed to the senior ranks in 1938–39 whilst with Bohemians, winning seven full caps – a total which no doubt would have been much greater had the war not intervened. A further three caps were added to the O'Flanagan tally in 1947 during his time at Highbury. In one of those fixtures, against England on 30 September, he lined up alongside his brother Michael, who, incidentally, was also an Irish international rugby player.

When his playing days finally came to an end in 1949, Dr O'Flanagan returned to a medical practice in his native Dublin and, hardly surprisingly given his sporting background, was offered the position as Irish team doctor for three Olympic Games. Such an accolade was richly deserved by this versatile and accomplished sportsman.

KEVIN O'FLANAGAN'S ARSENAL CAREER RECORD

SEASON	FOOTBALL LEAGUE		F.A. CUP		F.L. CUP		EUROPE		TOTAL	
	Apps.	Goals	Apps.	Goals	Apps.	Goals	Apps.	Goals	Apps.	Goals
1945–46			2						2	
1946–47	14	3							14	3
TOTAL	14	3	2						16	3

DAVID O'LEARY

Born: London, 2 May 1958
Signed for Arsenal: June 1973
League Debut: v Burnley (A) August 1975

David O'Leary has provided an enduring link between Arsenal and Ireland for almost 20 years now. His story is more than worthy of a book in itself, and any attempt to do justice to the man in the limited space available here will prove a very difficult task. In sixteen seasons as a professional, David has played under five different managers and has picked up every domestic honour the game has to offer. When the Gunners finally won the hitherto elusive League Championship title in 1989, after the most dramatic climax to a season ever, no player deserved to bask in Arsenal's glory more than Ireland's David O'Leary.

Born in Stoke Newington, London, David returned to Ireland as an infant with his family. As a 12-year-old he was a member of Shelbourne's junior team and spent the next five years progressing through the various ranks of the Dublin club. It was while he was playing in 'Shels' youth team that O'Leary was 'discovered' by Arsenal's Irish scout, Bill Darby, who immediately alerted the Highbury club. Arsenal did not stand on ceremony, and in June 1973 the 15-year-old became an Arsenal apprentice. Two years later, he signed on the dotted line and became a fully-fledged Gunner.

Following a somewhat shaky start in the youth team, David found his feet in the reserves. In August 1975, just over three years after signing, manager Bertie Mee reckoned he had seen enough to justify O'Leary's inclusion in the first team for the opening game of the 1975–76 season. David never looked back and went on to become the bedrock around which Arsenal have built their defence for nigh on two decades. In those years, David has experienced the full range of emotions with his beloved Arsenal – the heartbreak of Cup final defeat on two occasions, the elation of Cup final victory and the ultimate euphoria of

League Championship success. He is currently Arsenal's longest serving player and to date he has made an incredible 673 appearances in an Arsenal shirt, eclipsing George Armstrong's club record of 607 matches in first class competitions.

It was in the 1977–78 season that the Irish connection at Highbury really gelled. O'Leary and fellow Irishman Sammy Nelson topped the league appearance chart with 41 games apiece. He, alongside Pat Jennings, Pat Rice, John Devine, Liam Brady, Frank Stapleton and Jim Harvey, helped the Gunners achieve their best league position since 1973, coming fifth. They also reached their first major Cup final since 1972. It was in that 1978 FA Cup final that David experienced his first major disappointment, as the Gunners went down by a single goal to Ipswich Town. However, amends were made exactly a year later when Arsenal returned to Wembley, this time to take on Manchester United in the final tie. The Gunners, after forfeiting a two-goal cushion, clinched the tie in the dying seconds and the bitter memories of the previous year were quickly erased.

The 1979–80 season promised so much for O'Leary and his six fellow Irishmen in the side. However, when trophies were being awarded at the finale, the 'green Gunners' were once again the nearly men. They finished a respectable fourth in the league but were denied at the death in major cup competitions. They met West Ham in their third successive FA Cup final only to lose unexpectedly to the Second Division side. Matters were exacerbated by the defeat by Valencia in the European Cup Winners Cup final just four days after the disappointment at Wembley. Following that frustrating 1979–80 season, Arsenal's Irish connection began gradually to disintegrate. Brady left for Juventus, Stapleton for Manchester United and Rice was transferred to Watford. But O'Leary was adamant that he would remain at Highbury, displaying a loyalty to his club that is all too rare in today's game. That loyalty was rewarded when he was appointed captain at the beginning of 1980–81.

By the time Arsenal made it to Wembley again, this time to face Liverpool in the 1987 League Cup final, O'Leary had clocked up over four hundred league appearances and was the only sur-

David O'Leary (photo: Irish Post)

vivor from the previous three Wembley visits. The Gunners were victorious in this particular collision between two of the juggernauts of English soccer, running out 2–1 winners after extra-time.

Arsenal contested the final of the same competition the following year against what could be considered lesser opposition in the form of Luton Town. O'Leary missed the final through injury and his dominating presence in the centre of defence was sorely missed as the Gunners lost the tie by 2–3 to the Hatters.

Every professional footballer's lifetime ambition is to win a Championship medal and David O'Leary was no different. Only a small proportion achieve that ultimate goal and David had to wait fourteen seasons for his finest hour; and it was worth waiting for. The Gunners, having led the table for most of the 1988–89 season, somehow managed to throw away four points in their last two home games, leaving themselves the mountainous task of travelling to Fortress Anfield for the final game of the season, needing to win by two clear goals to clinch the title on goal difference. No one gave them a chance and who could blame them? Could anyone remember the last side to beat Liverpool at

Anfield, never mind win by two goals? A goalless first half seemed to tip the balance even more in favour of the Merseysiders. Alan Smith's second-half strike gave the visitors a glimmer of hope. But as the final seconds ticked away Arsenal's relentless bombardment of the Liverpool goal seemed to have been in vain. With the game in injury time, the cause looked well and truly lost, until Michael Thomas swept the ball past the advancing Grobbelar with almost the last kick of the game. The euphoria which followed knew no bounds, tears flowed freely and David O'Leary, the old man of the team, had finally achieved his ultimate ambition.

In 1989–90 David added a further 34 league appearances to his match tally and when he came on as a substitute for Steve Bould against Norwich in the final game of the season, he surpassed George Armstrong's record of 500 league appearances. The 1990–91 campaign was one of trial and tribulation for O'Leary. After reporting late for pre-season training following an exhausting and draining World Cup in Italy, David was disciplined by Arsenal supremo George Graham, who insisted O'Leary should train with the reserves as punishment. For Arsenal's most loyal and selfless servant to be treated in such a way was despicable to say the least – even more so when one considers that Paul Gascoigne and Gary Lineker were granted extended leave from White Hart Lane following their World Cup endeavours with England. And when Andy Linigan arrived at Highbury, it looked as if O'Leary's career at Arsenal was all but over. This was not to be, however, and what those two incidents did was to illustrate graphically the high regard in which O'Leary is held throughout the football world; enquiries from other clubs began to flood into Highbury: Leeds United, Manchester City, Crystal Palace and Derby County all wanted him. So did George Graham though, and so O'Leary remained. He has since seen off the challenge of Linigan, just as he has done with no fewer than twenty other pretenders to his throne over the years, and has displayed a versatility in his game not previously seen, excelling at right-back or as a sweeper as well as in his own recognised central defensive role. David is once again very much a part of the Arsenal set-up and when he collected the second championship medal of his career at the end of the 1990–91 season, the early season events seemed but a minor blip on the graph of his truly illustrious Arsenal career.

On the international front O'Leary has displayed the same level of commitment and loyalty to his country as he has to his club over the years. He has been an Irish international for longer than he has been a Gunner, captaining both the Schoolboy and Youth sides before winning his first full cap against England in 1977. To date he has amassed a total of 55 caps, a tally which would have been much greater had Jack Charlton not left him out of the side for two years, following a row remarkably similar to the one which blighted his Arsenal career. Again, as in the Graham

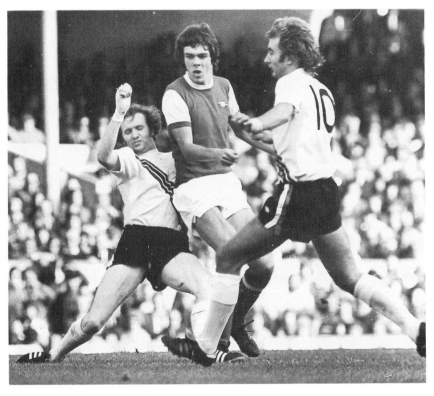

David O'Leary wins a tackle against Stoke in 1976 (photo: Irish Post)

incident, O'Leary was the innocent party and was unfairly punished. The highlight of David's international career was the 1990 World Cup finals in Italy, the enduring memory of which will be the sight of him falling to his knees in jubilation after scoring the penalty against Romania which took Ireland into the quarter-finals of the World Cup for the first time ever.

David O'Leary is the complete professional, a model for all young players, and has been one of Ireland's and Arsenal's greatest ambassadors. In February 1991 he signed a new two year deal which means he will see out his playing days at Highbury, something that means more to O'Leary than any amount of money or medals.

DAVID O'LEARY'S ARSENAL CAREER RECORD

SEASON	FOOTBALL LEAGUE		F.A. CUP		F.L. CUP		EUROPE		TOTAL	
	Apps.	Goals	Apps.	Goals	Apps.	Goals	Apps.	Goals	Apps.	Goals
1975–76	27		1		2				30	
1976–77	33	2	3		4	1			40	3
1977–78	41	1	6	1	6				53	2
1978–79	37	2	11		1		5		54	2
1979–80	34	1	9		6		9		58	1
1980–81	24	1	1		2				27	1
1981–82	40	1	1		5		4		50	1
1982–83	36	1	5		7		2		50	1
1983–84	36		1		4				41	
1984–85	36		3		3				42	
1985–86	35		5		7				47	
1986–87	39		4		9				52	
1987–88	23		4		6	1			33	1
1988–89	26		2						28	
1989–90	28(6)	1	3		4				35(6)	1
1990–91	11(9)	1	5(1)		1				17(10)	1
TOTAL	506(15)	11	64(1)	1	67	2	20		657(16)	14

Substitute Appearances in Brackets

FRANK O'NEILL

Born: Dublin, 13 April 1940
Signed for Arsenal: April 1959
League Debut: v Nottingham Forest (A) December 1960

Frank O'Neill joined Arsenal from Dublin's famous soccer nursery, Home Farm in April 1959. Home Farm have, over the years, built up a reputation for supplying quality players to the top English league sides. These include the present-day Liverpool captain, Ronnie Whelan, as well as former Manchester United stars Johnny Giles and Mick Martin, to name but a few. Therefore the Gunners had good reason to feel optimistic about their new acquisition. On this occasion, however, Arsenal could consider themselves somewhat unlucky in comparison with their great northern rivals, as their signing didn't match up to expectations. O'Neill had been regarded as a wing half of considerable ability as a teenager, hence Arsenal's decision to sign him as a professional.

Frank made his debut for the Gunners in a thrilling eight-goal encounter with Nottingham Forest at the City Ground on New Year's Eve 1960. Arsenal ran out 5–3 winners, but O'Neill failed to impress enough to guarantee himself regular first team football. His name appeared on the team sheet just once more, for the game against Blackpool in April 1961. Again the Gunners were victorious, but that game signalled the end of Frank O'Neill's brief flirtation with the Arsenal first team. By the beginning of 1961–62 he was back in his native Dublin plying his trade with Shamrock Rovers.

Frank's Rovers career provided enough reward to erase the bitter memories of his comparatively unsuccessful time with Arsenal. In 13 seasons at Milltown he scored 87 league goals, won a League Championship medal in 1964, and in 1970 was appointed player-manager. Furthermore, he gained international recognition by winning his first cap against Czechoslovakia in 1962, and collected a further 19 in an international career which spanned ten years. In 1974 Frank joined Rovers' League of Ireland rivals, Waterford United.

NIALL QUINN

Born: Dublin, 6 October 1966
Signed for Arsenal: November 1983
League Debut: v Liverpool (H) December 1985

Niall Quinn could have made it to the top in any one of five team sports. As a teenager he shone at Ireland's traditional sports of hurling and Gaelic football. He appeared for Dublin Minors in the 1983 All-Ireland hurling Minor final, and when Dublin College's GAA team toured Australia, young Niall was appointed team captain. It was during that tour that he was offered a contract to play Australian Rules football, an offer which would have netted him £100,000 a year. Not surprisingly for a man towering at 6ft 5in, he also tried his hand at basketball. But Niall turned his back on all these sports to concentrate his energies on soccer.

Discovered by Arsenal's Irish scout, Bill Darby, the lanky hopeful made a significant impression in his trials at Highbury and in 1983 he signed on the dotted line as a professional for Arsenal. In December 1986 an injury to the Gunners' established striker, Tony Woodcock, gave Quinn an early opportunity to prove his worth in the first team. Though still a raw teenager, the presence of the mighty Liverpool at Highbury held no fear for Quinn: on the contrary, he had an inspired debut and marked the occasion with a goal – the first Arsenal strike in four league games. Charlie Nicholas added another to secure both points for the homesters.

Niall managed just nine more full appearances in that 1985–86 season, each time standing in for Woodcock, but failed to add to his goal tally. He began the 1986–87 season as first choice centre-forward, having an unbroken run of 33 league appearances and playing a vital role, with half a dozen goals, in a run of 17 consecutive league games in which the Gunners remained undefeated. But the impressive sequence came to an end at Old Trafford in January 1987 when high-flying Arsenal went down 2–0 to Manchester United. That defeat signalled a decline just as dramatic as the rise which had gone before. A run of nine games without a victory and only two goals scored (including one from Quinn which earned Arsenal a draw at Sheffield Wednesday) set the alarm bells ringing. Drastic measures were required and Niall Quinn became the scapegoat. He was dropped in April and never regained a regular first team place.

In 1987–88 Niall made just eleven first team appearances, five of them as a substitute, and to compound matters he suffered an indignity known to few professional footballers: he came on in one game as a substitute, only to be substituted himself later in the same game. For the next two years Quinn languished in the Arsenal Reserves, unable to get into the first team and having numerous transfer requests turned down. He earned a recall in October 1989 and made half a dozen consecutive appearances, scoring two goals, which helped take the Gunners to the top of the table. But at the end of that particular run Quinn was dropped once more and never appeared for the Gunners in the league again. He played his last game in an Arsenal shirt against Stoke in the FA Cup in January 1990, presenting Arsenal with what was to be a welcome farewell present by scoring the only goal of the game.

In March 1990, almost four months after his final first team game, Quinn joined Manchester City for £700,000 and immediately repaid City manager Howard Kendall's faith by scoring on his debut, and hitting a further three goals in nine league outings which effectively saved City from relegation. The move to City has revitalised Niall's career and he seems to be coming of age as a player. His strength has always been in the air, but recently he has been displaying all the characteristics of an outstanding striker in the making. An encouraging deftness of touch at ground level, combined with poise and confidence, has brought him an impressive haul of 20 league goals in his first full season at Maine Road. His progress hasn't gone unnoticed. In March 1991 he signed a new contract with the club which will keep him in Manchester until 1996, and in May he was voted 'Player of the Season' by the Manchester City Supporters' Club.

Niall has represented his country at Youth, Under 21, 'B' and full levels and seems to be a jinx on the fortunes of England. Having met them seven times at different levels, he has never been

Niall Quinn (photo: Bill Smith Photography)

on the losing side. In fact it was his brace of goals in the 4–1 demolition of England 'B' at Cork in 1990 which earned him his seat on the plane to Italy for the 1990 World Cup Finals. In Italy he became one of the stars in Jack Charlton's great adventure by scoring the equalising goal against Holland which earned Ireland a place in the second phase. His rapid progress has been such that Niall is now firmly established as Ireland's first choice centre-forward, the position vacated in October 1990 (after 14 years' sterling service) by another ex-Gunner, Frank Stapleton.

To date, Quinn has accumulated 21 caps – 12 of which were won during his time as a Gunner – and on present form looks set to add many more to that tally.

NIALL QUINN'S ARSENAL CAREER RECORD

SEASON	FOOTBALL LEAGUE		F.A. CUP		F.L. CUP		EUROPE		TOTAL	
	Apps.	Goals	Apps.	Goals	Apps.	Goals	Apps.	Goals	Apps.	Goals
1985–86	10(2)	1	2(1)		2				14(3)	1
1986–87	35	8	4	1	9	3			48	12
1987–88	6(5)	2	1(1)		1(2)				8(8)	2
1988–89	2(1)	1							2(1)	1
1989–90	6	2	1	1	2	1			9	4
TOTAL	59(8)	14	8(2)	2	14(2)	4			81(12)	20

Substitute Appearances in Brackets

FRANK RANSOM

Born: Ireland c. 1882
Signed for Woolwich Arsenal: August 1900
League Debut: v Leicester Fosse (A) December 1903

Having previously been on the books of Tottenham Hotspur as a junior, Frank Ransom spent five years with Arsenal, but managed just one league appearance in all that time.

He made over two hundred appearances in Arsenal's junior and reserve sides, however, and was comfortable in any of the defensive positions.

Ransom replaced Roddy McEachrane at centre-half on Boxing Day, 1903, and made his one and only first team appearance for Arsenal in a goalless draw against Leicester Fosse.

In June 1905 he was transferred to junior side Southern United where he stayed for just one season. Frank joined Crystal Palace, his last known league club, in 1906. He played in just four reserve team fixtures for the Eagles, the last of them in January 1907.

PAT RICE

Born: Belfast, 17 March 1949
Signed for Arsenal: December 1964
League Debut: v Burnley(A) December 1967

Born in Belfast on St Patrick's Day, 1949, Pat Rice moved with his family to London as a schoolboy ten years later. The Rice family set up their new home just 200 yards from the famous Highbury stadium and almost from that day, young Pat was determined that one day he would become a Gunner. He was just 15 years old when Arsenal took him on as an apprentice, and in March 1966 he signed on as a professional. To begin with, there were those at the club who felt that he would not make the grade. How wrong they were. What Pat lacked in skill was more than compensated for by his single-minded determination to play for the club he had idolised since boyhood. His dedication to duty was a lesson for all; at one stage he almost took up residence at Highbury, giving up his free afternoons to get in extra training and to work on the weaker aspects of his game. The reward for such dedication came in 1968 when, as a member of Arsenal's FA Youth Cup winning team, he picked up the first of the cluster of medals which he was to win as an Arsenal player. His perseverance really paid off in 1967–68 when he was given his first opportunity in the first team, coming on as a substitute for future Highbury supremo George Graham, in the 0–1 away defeat at Burnley. Pat made another five appearances that season (including three as a substitute). Next season, due mainly to the consistency of Peter Storey at right-back, Rice did not get a game. He began the 1969–70 league campaign with a run of five games at right-back, but once again he lost his place to Storey and was restricted to only two more games that season.

By the beginning of the historic double-winning season, 1970–71, it was felt that Rice had progressed sufficiently to justify regular first team football. Once again he began the season at right-back, only this time he kept his place throughout. In that,

Pat Rice (photo: Bill Smith Photography)

the most momentous season in the history of Arsenal Football Club, Rice missed only one league game and appeared in all FA Cup games including the final against Liverpool which the Gunners won 2–1 after extra-time. They thus joined arch-rivals Spurs as the only clubs to accomplish the elusive 'double' this century.

Thereafter Pat became a fixture in the side, missing only a handful of league games over the next nine years. All in all, he amassed a total of 397 league appearances, played in 67 FA Cup games (a club record) and played 27 times for the Gunners in European competition, creating yet another record for the club.

In 1977 Pat's ultimate dream came true when he was appointed captain of his beloved Arsenal. As team skipper, he was a natural, displaying to everyone those priceless qualities of leadership and motivation which led the club to three successive Cup finals in 1978, 1979 and 1980, and to the European Cup Winners' Cup final also in 1980.

When he led his team out to face Ipswich in the 1978 FA Cup final, Rice was the only survivor from the double-winning side of 1971, and from the team which lost to Leeds United in the 1972 Wembley showdown. Although the Gunners lost the 1978 final, they were back the following year and, after the unforgettable classic battle with Manchester United, Pat Rice joined that exclusive club of Irishmen who have held aloft the FA Cup: legendary figures such as Jackie Carey and Danny Blanchflower to name but two. Pat made his record-breaking fifth cup final appearance in 1980 against West Ham but for the third time in his career had to be content with a runners' up medal. Disappointment at that defeat was to be exacerbated four days later, when Graham Rix's missed spot kick gave the European Cup Winners Cup to Valencia.

The 1980–81 season began with Pat as club captain but unable to get into the side. David O'Leary took over the captaincy and another Dubliner, John Devine, took over the right-back berth, restricting Rice to only two substitute appearances in what turned out to be his last season as an Arsenal player. In November 1980, almost exactly sixteen years after arriving, Pat Rice left Highbury to join Second Division Watford. He helped Watford achieve Division One status for the first time in their history in 1983, and then he returned to Arsenal in the summer of 1984 as Youth team coach. In 1988, exactly 20 years after he had won an FA Youth Cup Winners' medal, he guided his youth charges to victory in the same competition.

Although he speaks with a Cockney accent, Pat Rice was totally committed to the N. Ireland cause, and with Sammy Nelson, he formed the exciting, overlapping full-back partnership which served Arsenal and N. Ireland so loyally and consistently throughout the 1970s. As a Gunner, Pat won two Under–23 caps, as well as his first full cap in a match against Israel in 1968, long before he had broken into the Arsenal first XI! A further 48 caps were added to his tally in the years that followed and appropriately enough he won all of them as an Arsenal player.

PAT RICE'S ARSENAL CAREER RECORD

SEASON	FOOTBALL LEAGUE		F.A. CUP		F.L. CUP		EUROPE		TOTAL	
	Apps.	Goals	Apps.	Goals	Apps.	Goals	Apps.	Goals	Apps.	Goals
1967–68	2(4)				1				3(4)	
1968–69										
1969–70	7	1			1		1		9	1
1970–71	41		9		5		8		63	
1971–72	42	1	9	1	4		6		61	2
1972–73	39	2	7		4				50	2
1973–74	41	1	3		1				45	1
1974–75	32		8						40	
1975–76	42	1	1		2				45	1
1976–77	42	3	3		6				51	3
1977–78	38	2	6		7				51	2
1978–79	39	1	11		1		´6		57	1
1979–80	26		10		4		5(1)		45(1)	
1980–81	0(2)								0(2)	
TOTAL	391(6)	12	67	1	36		26(1)		520(7)	13

Substitute Appearances in Brackets

TOMMY SHANKS

Born: New Ross, Co. Wexford, 1880
Signed for Woolwich Arsenal: January 1903
League Debut (for Arsenal): v Port Vale, January 1903

One of the most renowned inside forwards of his day, the diminutive Tommy Shanks spent over a decade in the Football League with no fewer than seven clubs. After leaving Wexford to join Derby West End in the latter part of the nineteenth century, he proceeded to go through clubs with almost the same regularity as he was to go through frustrated defenders who stood in his path. Although he did not stay long with any one club, however, on his departure he invariably left behind supporters and management alike bemoaning his absence.

Shanks' career began in earnest when he left Derby West End for their more illustrious First Division neighbours Derby County in 1898. He spent three seasons with the Rams before signing for Brentford in November 1901. Ten goals in 36 games for the Southern League side was enough to convince Arsenal that Shanks was the man they needed to take them into the First Division. He was, however, generally regarded as Brentford's most gifted player, and they were not prepared to let him go without a fight. Despite rumblings of discontent among the Bees fans, however, Arsenal made Brentford an offer they couldn't refuse. In return for the services of Shanks, Brentford received a club record fee of £200 plus Arsenal's Irish inside forward Maurice Connor.

Tommy played his first match for the Gunners in the 1–1 draw away at Port Vale in January 1903. He failed to mark his debut with a goal, but made up for any disappointment when he played his first home game for his new club, scoring twice in the Gunners' 4–0 thrashing of Burnley and so paying off a large chunk of his transfer fee. Not completely familiar with his new surroundings and team-mates, Shanks managed to find the net on only two more occasions that season. However, more significantly, out of the 14 league fixtures he appeared in for the Gunners that season,

Tommy Shanks finished on the losing side just once! Although it was their best season since their election to the Football League in 1893, it still wasn't enough to take them into the top flight.

By the beginning of the 1903–04 season, Tommy was feeling much more comfortable in his new surroundings, and did it show! The Gunners began the new campaign like a steamroller, with Tommy Shanks at the controls. They won their first eight games – scoring an incredible 35 goals against just 3 conceded – and did not drop a point until the last day of October 1903! By the end of the season Shanks was the Gunners' top scorer on 24 goals, including three hat-tricks and four in one game – a feat he had also achieved in an FA Cup match as a Brentford player.

Tommy's 24 league goals were enough to take the Gunners into Division One for the first time ever, but by the time the curtain was raised on the new season in September 1904, the star of the show had long since departed. Almost immediately the 1903–04 season ended, he was on his way back to Griffin Park and Brentford.

Tommy continued at Brentford as if he had never been away. Fifty three appearances in his first two seasons back with the club produced 17 goals, taking his league tally overall to 64 goals in 159 outings. Nevertheless, things soon turned sour, and for the second time in three years Tommy Shanks was to leave Brentford under a shroud of controversy. The 1906–07 season began badly for Shanks. He played in Brentford's first three games of the season and although the Bees recorded victories in two of these matches, it was decided that Shanks was not performing to the high standards that were expected of him. Consequently, for the fourth game, he was dropped. This precipitated strike action by the player, and led to his requesting a transfer. Brentford's directors did everything they could in an effort to get him to remain, but the player was adamant that he wanted to leave, and in October 1906 was transferred to Leicester Fosse, the team against whom he had scored his first Arsenal hat-trick. The fee of £275 was split between Brentford and Arsenal, the former receiving £125 with the Gunners collecting the remaining £150.

Fosse's position was similar to Arsenal's in the days before

Shanks – bravely battling for First Division status since their election to the Football League. Once again Shanks proved to be the vital piece in the jigsaw. Generally acknowledged as the man who guided Fosse into Division One for the first time ever, he capped his stay at Filbert Street by scoring the winning goal in the crucial promotion decider at Stoke in 1908. Tommy left Filbert Street in 1909 to return to London and Leyton, and ended his illustrious if somewhat chequered career with Clapton Orient, the team he joined in 1911.

Tommy Shanks was regarded as one of the best players of his age and will certainly go down in history as the man who almost single-handedly took two different clubs into Division One for the first time. An Irish international on three occasions, twice as a Gunner, he lined up alongside Maurice Connor, the man he replaced at Arsenal, on a night in 1903 when they both made their debuts for Ireland in a match against Scotland. Although the Irish had never before defeated the Scots, they were victorious on that occasion and went on to a share in the Home International Championships for the first time.

TOMMY SHANKS' ARSENAL CAREER RECORD

SEASON	FOOTBALL LEAGUE		F.A. CUP		F.L. CUP		EUROPE		TOTAL	
	Apps.	Goals	Apps.	Goals	Apps.	Goals	Apps.	Goals	Apps.	Goals
1902–03	14	4							14	4
1903–04	30	24	4	1					34	25
TOTAL	44	28	4	1					48	29

JOSHUA WALTER SLOAN

Born: Lurgan, 30 April 1920
Signed for Arsenal: May 1946
League Debut (for Arsenal): v Wolves (A) August 1946

Of all the professional footballers labelled wandering minstrels, Joshua Sloan is the king of them all. In just over a decade in the game, he appeared for no fewer than 15 different clubs, seldom staying with any one of them for more than a season.

Like several other Irish Gunners, Sloan first laced up his boots with Irish League club Glenavon. In 1937 he joined Manchester United with whom he stayed a couple of seasons, without getting a first team game. He left Old Trafford for Tranmere Rovers in 1939, and then spent the last war season, 1944–45, with Fulham, playing 11 games and managing a hat-trick against Brentford in March 1944. He returned to Tranmere for the 1945–46 season and joined Arsenal in May 1946.

Sloan made his debut for the Gunners at inside forward against Wolverhampton Wanderers at Molineux. That first game of the 1946–47 season turned out to be an entirely forgettable affair – Wolves thrashed the Gunners 6–1. He made a total of 30 league appearances for Arsenal that season, including an unbroken run of 25 games at wing half. Next season, Joshua failed to make a significant enough impression to guarantee regular first team football and, after managing just three league games all season, he was transferred to Sheffield United in February 1948. Again, his stay with his new club was a short one. Less than six months after arriving at Bramall Lane he was off again, this time to try his luck in Italy with Brescia, becoming one of the pioneers of the now well-worn Italian trail. However, his new surroundings failed to provide him with any degree of stability and during his three-year stint in Italy he appeared in the colours of no fewer than four different clubs.

He left Brescia after only four months to join Milan FC, and nine months later, in August 1949, Joshua signed for Torino.

112

Exactly a year later he was on the books of Udine. Sloan's Italian adventure turned full circle when he rejoined Brescia in 1951. This did not last for long, however, because later the same year he returned to Britain to play for Norwich City in a deal costing the Canaries something in the region of 7 million lire. But the transfer was not without complications: representatives of Brescia and Norwich met in a Paris hotel in December 1951 in circumstances which must have resembled a scene from an old Marx Brothers' movie. The Italian vendors spoke Italian, German and French but couldn't converse in English; the English investors spoke in only their native tongue, while the French bank manager spoke English, Spanish and French but no Italian, and the interpreter spoke only French and Italian. Somehow they managed to break down the language barriers and the deal which took Sloan to Carrow Road was struck. It hardly seemed worth the trouble when the following year Sloan was plying his trade in the colours of Peterborough United! But still he refused to settle, and in July 1954 he was appointed player-coach with Maltese club Rabat. In September 1955 he took up a similar post with Hastings United; in March 1956 he became player-manager of Lockheed and in August 1956 he became player-coach at Bath City. In 1963 Joshua's travels took him to Australia where he became coach to Melbourne club Juventus. He settled in Australia and was later appointed Chairman of the National Soccer Coaches Association.

As a player with more clubs than Ronan Rafferty, it seems appropriate that Sloan was one of the select band of players to appear for both 'Irelands' at international level. In 1946 he was honoured twice by the Republic, and the following year he made one appearance for N. Ireland. All three caps were won during his sojourn at Highbury.

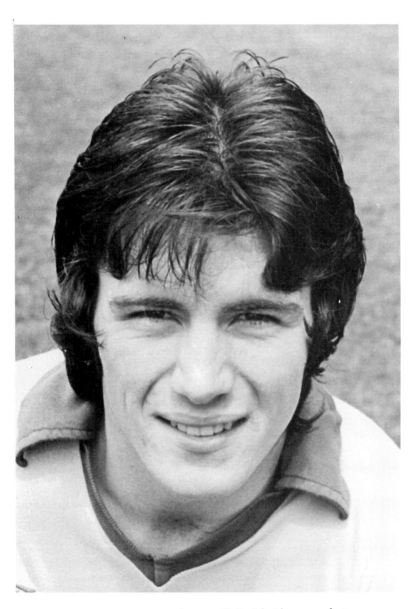

Frank Stapleton (photo: Bill Smith Photography)

FRANK STAPLETON

Born: Dublin, 10 July 1956
Signed for Arsenal: June 1972
League Debut: v Stoke City (H) March 1975

Born in Harmonstown in Dublin, Frank Stapleton, like so many of his compatriots who later became soccer stars in the Football League, learnt the basics of his trade playing the Gaelic code in Ireland. Stapleton's first experience of the cut and thrust world of professional football came in 1972 when, as an impressionable 16-year-old, he had unsuccessful trials with Manchester United. But Frank's disappointment at the rejection by United soon turned to joy when, in June of the same year, Arsenal stepped in to sign him as an apprentice professional. He signed full pro forms with the Gunners the following year and, with over 100 goals in all competitions over the next half a dozen seasons, Arsenal's gain was very much Manchester United's loss – so much so that the Lancashire giants ultimately paid Arsenal £900,000 for the man they could have had for nothing nine years previously!

Frank made his league debut in March 1975 in the 1–1 home draw with Stoke City. It was his only outing that season, but next season he was ready to join fellow countrymen Pat Rice, Sammy Nelson, Terry Mancini, David O'Leary and Liam Brady as a regular part of the first team set-up. Twenty-three league appearances that year produced a disappointing return of only four goals. However, the arrival of 'Supermac' Malcolm McDonald from Newcastle United in the summer of 1976 worked wonders for Stapleton in the new league campaign. The two strikers struck up an excellent understanding and Big Frank ended the season with a tally of 13 league goals. From that time on, the goals flowed for Stapleton. He was Arsenal's leading scorer with 17 goals in 1978–79, joint-top scorer with Alan Sunderland in 1979–80, both finishing on 14 apiece, and top again with 14 in 1980–81. By the end of 1981, Stapleton had a total of 75 league goals under his belt and was widely regarded as one of the best centre-forwards

115

in the business. He had no peers in the air and many of his goals came from powerfully propelled headers. He worked hard at other relatively weaker aspects of his game, so that by 1981 when he left Highbury, he had blossomed into a finely-tuned, highly-polished, first-class marksman.

The big man was just as prolific in cup games as in league matches, and his 14 goals in 27 games between 1977 and 1980 played a major part in Arsenal's three-year cup-run during that period. Stapleton appeared in all three finals, picking up a loser's medal in 1978 and 1980 and a winner's medal in 1979, scoring a goal in the latter and contributing to the 3–2 nail-biting defeat of Manchester United. He also played in the European Cup Winners' Cup final against Valencia in 1980, adding another loser's medal to his collection.

Stapleton was named Arsenal's 'Player of the Year' in 1977 and again in 1980, so that when he left Arsenal in the summer of 1981 the Highbury faithful were understandably more than a little perturbed. They knew that this was no ordinary player they were losing and that he would be very difficult to replace. The fans apportioned the blame for their star striker's departure equally between the player and the club. It was felt that the club did not do enough to keep Stapleton at Highbury; on the other hand, Stapleton's contract with Arsenal was up and he felt the time was ripe for a new challenge and was determined to leave at all costs.

When news of Frank's desire to leave Arsenal broke, the rush for his signature began. Offers came from Italy and West Germany and the player began serious talks with Liverpool. However, it was Manchester United supremo Ron Atkinson who won the day. He persuaded Stapleton that his future lay at Old Trafford, and so, after a lot of soul-searching, Frank Stapleton agreed to become a Manchester United player. The major wrangle in the transfer was the size of the fee. Arsenal thought he was worth £1.5 million whereas United's estimate was £750,000. As the two clubs could not agree, the whole affair was left in the hands of the Football League Appeals Committee, which valued Stapleton at £900,000. United, unable to disguise their eagerness, paid immediately. Atkinson was delighted to get the man he had always regarded as one of the best strikers in the league. He was not to be disappointed. Stapleton soon built up a fine understanding with his new striking partners, heading United's scoring list in each of his first three seasons with the club. In six seasons with United he made a total of 265 appearances, scoring 78 goals, and made the familiar trip to Wembley Stadium on four more occasions.

Another loser's medal was added to his ever growing collection following the League Cup final defeat by Liverpool in 1983. He won FA Cup Winners' medals with United following their victories over Brighton in 1983 and Everton in 1985. When he scored against Brighton in '83, he became the first player ever to score in the final for two different FA Cup winning teams.

In March 1986, as a reward for long and loyal service, Stapleton was given a free transfer to Ajax Amsterdam. Unfortunately, however, his time with the Dutch club was an unhappy one: he was dogged by back trouble and, after manager Johan Cruyff moved to Barcelona, he found himself out of favour and returned to Derby County.

At 32 Stapleton found himself without a club, though still registered by Ajax and training with Manchester City, until French club Le Havre saved the day with the offer of a two-year contract. However, he failed to settle in France, returning to Britain in 1989 to join the playing staff of Blackburn Rovers, with whom he spent two seasons. In April 1991, at the age of 35, he was given a free transfer, and at the time of writing is still without a club.

A former Eire School and Youth international, Frank won his first full cap against Turkey in October 1976 and marked his debut with a goal. He won 24 caps while playing for Arsenal, and to date has a total of 71. In May 1990 he scored his 20th international goal in Ireland's pre-World Cup friendly against Malta, breaking his country's all-time goal scoring record set by Don Givens in 1980. The highlight of his international career was captaining Ireland in the 1988 European Championships. Inevitably, in recent times he has not been as effective as of old, lacking pace with age and now playing deeper at times. In November 1988 he asked to be dropped from the World Cup qualifying match with Northern Ireland. It was the first time since he was capped that the 33-year-old striker had been left out, and in October 1990, the old veteran announced his retirement from the international scene.

For club and country alike, Frank Stapleton has been a great servant; an unselfish striker and a tirelessly working target man, he was rewarded with a testimonial in Dublin in May 1988.

FRANK STAPLETON'S ARSENAL CAREER RECORD

SEASON	FOOTBALL LEAGUE		F.A. CUP		F.L. CUP		EUROPE		TOTAL	
	Apps.	Goals	Apps.	Goals	Apps.	Goals	Apps.	Goals	Apps.	Goals
1974–75	1								1	
1975–76	23(2)	4	1		1(1)	1			25(3)	5
1976–77	40	13	3	1	6	3			49	17
1977–78	39	13	5	4	7	2			51	19
1978–79	41	17	11	6	1	1	6	4	59	28
1979–80	39	14	11	4	7	5	9		66	23
1980–81	40	14	1		4	2			45	16
TOTAL	223(2)	75	32	15	26(1)	14	15	4	296(3)	108

Substitute Appearances in Brackets

PETER TILLEY

Born: Lurgan, 13 January 1930
Signed for Arsenal: May 1952
League Debut: v Chelsea (H) September 1953

Of all the Irishmen who began their league careers at Highbury, Peter Tilley's has to be the shortest of them all. He signed for the Gunners from junior club Witton Athletic in May 1952 and spent 18 months at Highbury, managing just one league appearance in all that time. Standing in at centre-forward for Doug Lishman, who was the club's expert marksman of the day, Peter made his one and only appearance in an Arsenal shirt in the club's seventh league game of the 1953–54 season. With the Gunners still searching for their first victory of the campaign, it was hoped that Peter would bring some of the proverbial luck of the Irish to the proceedings. It was not to be, however, as the Gunners went down 1–2 at home to Chelsea.

In November 1953 Tilley was sold to Second Division Bury for £4,000. He spent over four seasons with the Gigg Lane side, making 86 league appearances for them and scoring twelve goals. In July 1958 he was given a free transfer and subsequently joined Halifax Town. Halifax's intention was to utilise Peter's experience in guiding their reserve team's fortunes, but his form was such that he quickly became an invaluable asset to their first team. He served the Shaymen in both attack and defence during a five-year period which saw him make 184 appearances and score 17 goals. In 1963, after 271 appearances in the Football League, the genial Tilley left the Shay for non-league Mossley.

During his ten years as a professional footballer, Peter failed to attract the attention of the Irish international selectors. But years later, long after he had hung up his boots, he did gain international recognition – when he was chosen to represent England . . . at bowls!

119

JOSEPH TONER

Born: Castlewellan, Co. Down, 30 March 1894
Signed for Arsenal: August 1919
League Debut: v Everton (A) October 1919

The 1919–20 league season saw Arsenal back in Division One after an absence of two years. The wind of change was blowing through Highbury and the new manager, Leslie Knighton, was entrusted with the task of building a team good enough to keep the Gunners in the top flight. The only problem was that he was expected to do it at minimal cost, and consequently Mr Knighton set about plundering the junior leagues throughout the British Isles. He met with quite a bit of success in the north of Ireland, where he initially acquired the services of Joseph Toner, who was later to be followed by Alex Mackie and Andy Kennedy.

Joe was signed from junior club Belfast United in the summer of 1919 and made his league debut against Everton in October of that year. By all accounts Toner had an exceptional debut at outside left in the 3–2 victory over the Merseysiders and consequently kept his place for the following ten games. But at the end of that sequence of matches, Joe found it difficult to get back into the side. It was to be 1924–25 (in what turned out to be his penultimate season with the club) before circumstances permitted him to put together another sequence of equal significance. In the intervening four seasons, he managed to claim a first team place on just 46 occasions.

Toner played in the opening two fixtures of 1925–26, bringing his final tally in an Arsenal shirt to exactly 100 games, before being transferred to St Johnstone.

He spent a couple of seasons in Scotland where he added a further two full N. Ireland caps to the half-dozen he had won as a Gunner. A broken leg forced the 5ft 7in winger into early retirement, whereupon he returned to Ireland. However, a year after sustaining the injury he returned to the game for a short period to play for Coleraine in the Irish League. Upon his retirement, Joseph Toner returned to his native Castlewellan where he died in November 1954.

JOSEPH TONER'S ARSENAL CAREER RECORD

SEASON	FOOTBALL LEAGUE		F.A. CUP		F.L. CUP		EUROPE		TOTAL	
	Apps.	Goals	Apps.	Goals	Apps.	Goals	Apps.	Goals	Apps.	Goals
1919–20	15	1	1						16	1
1920–21	12	3	1						13	3
1921–22	24	1	6						30	1
1922–23	7								7	
1923–24	3								3	
1924–25	26	1	3						29	1
1925–26	2								2	
TOTAL	89	6	11						100	6

ARSENAL'S IRISH MANAGERS

THEO FOLEY

Born: Dublin, 2 April 1937
Assistant Manager: 1986–May 1990

Theo Foley arrived at Highbury a few weeks after the appointment of his close friend George Graham as the Gunners' manager in May 1986. It was not the first time that the tough Scot and the genial Irishman had found themselves working in tandem towards a common goal: Foley had been Graham's assistant at Millwall, where they won the League Trophy in 1983, and they were the architects behind the Lions' promotion to Division Two in 1985. Before that, they were colleagues at QPR, so it came as no great surprise when the pair linked up once again at Highbury.

With Graham at the helm and Foley, his most trusted aide, as his Number Two, they set about plotting the break-up of the Merseyside monopoly. In their first season in charge they took the Gunners to a final fourth position in the league, their best placing since 1980. They also led the club to Wembley to face Liverpool in the League Cup final. When Ian Rush opened the scoring for Liverpool the old maxim that 'when Rush scores Liverpool don't lose' must have been prominent in everyone's mind. However, Charlie Nicholas's brace of goals in reply laid that particular ghost to rest forever and Highbury's new Celtic partnership picked up their first piece of silverware. The Gunners were back at Wembley the following year to face Luton Town in the same competition. In an open, exciting final the Londoners had to be content with runners' up medals as Luton won the tie by the odd goal in five.

The disappointment of that defeat was soon forgotten the following season as Arsenal pipped Liverpool to the League Championship in what must rate as the greatest finale to a league season ever. Few people gave the Gunners any chance when, having led the First Division for long periods, they found themselves in the seemingly impossible position of having to go to Anfield for the last game of the season, needing to win by two clear goals to

125

finish above the Merseyside masters on goal difference. As the last seconds ticked agonisingly away and with the Londoners leading through a second-half goal from Alan Smith, all seemed lost until Michael Thomas burst through to chip a shot over the flailing body of Liverpool 'keeper Grobbelar and into the net. The goal sent Arsenal's travelling hordes and players alike into a state of near delirium. And so for the first time since they won the double in 1971, Arsenal were crowned League Champions and Mr Graham and Mr Foley basked in the glory of the finest hour in their managerial careers.

Almost exactly a year after that triumph, Theo dropped something of a bombshell when he announced he was to quit the glamour of Highbury for the quiet backwater of Fourth Division Northampton Town. Even the Northampton chairman was amazed to get Theo to agree to take over the managerial reins at the County Ground. A touch of nostalgia may have been responsible for Theo's decision to turn his back on the bright lights of London, since his most successful and probably happiest days as a player had been spent at Northampton's County ground.

Like so many other gifted Dubliners, Theo Foley first laced up his boots with the city's famous football nursery – Home Farm. With Farm he matured into a fine, solid, fast-tackling right-back and in March 1955 he joined Exeter City, who were then playing in the old Division Three South. In May 1961, after 154 league outings with the Grecians, he joined Northampton and the six seasons he spent as captain with the Cobblers coincided with the most successful period in the club's 84-year history. They had just won promotion to the Third Division when Theo began playing with them. The following season, 1961–62, in which he was a permanent fixture, the Cobblers finished in eighth position and went on to win the division the season after that. Only two years later they scaled impossible heights and joined the First Division élite for the first time in their history. That 1965–66 season was to be the only one Northampton were to spend at the top and, unfortunately, their drop through the divisions was just as dramatic as their rise had been – by 1970 they were back in the Fourth! Foley had left the club in August 1967 to join Charlton

*Theo Foley, a successful manager for Arsenal
(photo: courtesy of Irish in Britain News)*

Athletic where he ended his playing career with half a dozen outings in 1967–68.

Capped nine times by the Republic, Theo got his first taste of management with the south Londoners before linking up with George Graham at Queens Park Rangers.

His decision to leave Highbury with still a year of his contract left to run came as a tremendous jolt to both George Graham and Arsenal. The club 'very reluctantly' let him go. Theo explained the reason for his abrupt departure: 'I was asked to take the Arsenal reserve side this season and I didn't fancy that. I wanted to be the boss again, but I didn't leave with any hard feelings: I had four marvellous years there'.

Theo's departure will leave a void at Highbury which will be very difficult to fill. A happy-go-lucky, exuberant character, he had struck up an excellent relationship with the Highbury staff and often played the role of 'middleman' between the manager and the players.

TERRY NEILL

Born: Belfast, May 1942
Manager: August 1976 – December 1983

In 1976, at the age of 34, Terry Neill was appointed Bertie Mee's successor to the Arsenal hot seat. He thus became one of the youngest managers in the club's history. Mee had been Arsenal's most successful manager in the post-war era, winning the European Fairs Cup in 1970 and, of course, leading the Gunners to the historic double in 1971, a feat for which he was awarded the title 'Manager of the Year'. Unfortunately, however, a decline was setting in at the club and in his last three seasons Arsenal finished 10th, 16th and 17th in the league, which was obviously not good enough for a club of Arsenal's stature. Consequently, when Terry Neill took charge, the club was in serious need of a programme of rebuilding and reorganisation. The fans were hungry for a quick return to the glory days and Neill had inherited a team in obvious decline. The big question was whether he could make the transformation from Arsenal player to Arsenal boss and take charge of men from his own generation, who only a few years earlier had been club colleagues.

Terry's career as a player began with Bangor in the Irish League. He moved to Highbury in December 1959, made 275 appearances for Arsenal in all competitions, and went on to become skipper. He served his managerial apprenticeship with Second Division Hull City, whom he joined as player-manager in June 1970. He was also appointed N. Ireland manager in the early '70s, and in September 1974, Neill succeeded Bill Nicholson as manager of Tottenham Hotspur. So when he returned to Highbury for the start of the 1976–77 league campaign, he had five years of managerial experience behind him and was therefore well prepared for his greatest challenge.

Terry began at Highbury as if he really meant business by paying Newcastle United a record transfer fee of £333,333 for 'Supermac' Malcolm McDonald. This turned out to be an excellent buy; McDonald scored 25 goals in his first season and he seemed to bring out the best in his new striking partner Frank Stapleton, who, after a stuttering start at the club, managed 13 goals that season. The Gunners finished 1976–77 in eighth position, a vast improvement on the previous season. The next season brought further improvement, with the Gunners finishing fifth in the league. But it was in the major cup competitions that Terry Neill excelled as a manager.

In 1978 the Gunners reached the semi-final of the League Cup, losing by the odd goal in three in a two-legged affair to Liverpool. They went one better in the FA Cup, only to lose 1–0 in the final to Ipswich Town. Neill took his team back to Wembley the following season and, after a cliff-hanging finish, ran out 3–2 winners over Manchester United. Terry Neill had won the first trophy of his career – either as a manager or a player! In May 1980 the Gunners were back at Wembley for their third successive FA Cup final appearance under the managership of Neill. But they had to be content with the runners-up spot once again after losing 1–0, this time to London rivals West Ham. The next week Arsenal went down 5–4 on penalties after 120 minutes' play had failed to produce a goal in the European Cup Winners' Final against Spanish cup-holders Valencia.

1980–81 witnessed steady progress in the club's quest for the League Championship, ending the campaign in third place, their best placing since 1973. In the seasons that followed Neill had to contend with the loss of some of his best players. Former 'Footballer of the Year' Liam Brady left for Juventus and Frank Stapleton, twice winner of Arsenal's 'Player of the Year' award, was sold to Manchester United. Neill's sorties into the transfer market to find replacements were not always successful and the club's fortunes once again began to decline.

In 1982–83, however, he was back on the trophy trail once again, reaching the semi-finals of both the League Cup and the FA Cup, only to lose in both contests to Manchester United. These defeats, coupled with a disappointing tenth league position, saw Neill come under considerable pressure. A particularly humiliating 2–1 home defeat by Third Division Walsall in the League

Cup in November 1983 all but finished Terry's managerial career at Highbury, and less than a month later he was sacked.

At a lesser club Neill's tenure of office might have been considered a very successful one; at a club of Arsenal's stature, however, one trophy in seven years is not considered good enough. Terry was more of an administrator than a manager, lacking the ruthless streak that is the mark of great leaders. The relative success that the club enjoyed only came about when Don Howe returned to Highbury as coach in 1977–78. Neill found it difficult to take charge of his old playing colleagues and made the cardinal error of washing his dirty linen in public. In the final analysis, however, it should be recognised that Neill was one of the Gunners' most successful post-war managers, never finishing out of the top ten in the league and frequently ending up in the top five during his seven-year stay.

Bill Darby, Arsenal's chief scout in Ireland

ARSENAL'S IRISH SCOUTS

It takes a rare talent to scrutinise schoolboys just into their teens and mark them out as future First Division and international players. However, at the helm of an extensive scouting network which covers practically every corner of Ireland, Arsenal have found two men who can perform such a task. Dublin-born Bill Darby and Belfast-born John Dillon have selflessly devoted the last twenty or so years of their lives to the search for new talent for Arsenal Football Club.

Mr Darby succeeded Mick Heron as the Gunners' Chief Scout in the Republic in 1968, and in the years since then has provided Arsenal FC with players of the calibre of Brady, Stapleton, Devine, O'Leary and Quinn – millions of pounds' worth of talent whose services Bill has acquired for the club for nothing. Nevertheless, his association with Arsenal got off to something of an uncertain start.

Bill acquired a love of the game both from his father (who had been a lifelong Arsenal supporter) and also whilst carrying out scouting duties on behalf of League of Ireland clubs Shelbourne, Longford and Drogheda. In the later '60s he travelled to London to try his luck with some of the big English clubs.

Soon after his arrival in the capital Gordon Clarke, Arsenal's chief scout, appointed Bill as their man in Dublin. Bill returned to his native city full of enthusiasm for his new vocation, and it wasn't long before he made his first discovery, a frail youngster called Liam Brady. Inexplicably, however, a few months later Bill was told his services were no longer required! But after Brady returned to Highbury for further trials the club again contacted Bill to reinstate him. Fortunately, he accepted and set about creating probably the most formidable scouting network of any English club in Ireland. He has gathered around him men with similar talents and abilities to his own in order to ensure no youngster of note slips through the net. In Dublin he is aided by an ex-Gunners favourite Joe Haverty, and with Pat Kelly and Tom Flynn in Waterford, Carl Humphries in Cork, Billy Kinane in Limerick (who is also manager of the City football team), this makes up Bill's team of Arsenal spies.

John Dillon was appointed Arsenal's chief scout in the north in 1970. Based in Belfast, he had spent the preceding twenty years as Liverpool's scout there. Mr Dillon's 'discoveries' do not come to mind quite as easily as Mr Darby's, probably due in no small part to the presence – until his death in June 1990 – of Manchester United's legendary Belfast scout Bob Bishop, who seemed to have a monopoly on all the young northern talent. Nevertheless, John is optimistic about the future and cites young Stephen Morrow, one of the Gunners reserve defenders, as an excellent future prospect. He also speaks very highly of his latest find, Mark McArdle, who arrived at Highbury this summer. John is aided in his endeavours by Noel Kivlehan who, as well as running the highly successful Moorfield Boys Team in his native Derry, casts an experienced eye over youngsters in the North-west.

ARSENAL'S ALL-TIME IRISH XI

In most circumstances in football it is an extremely difficult task to pick a team from a large squad of players. To choose Arsenal's all-time Irish XI from a pool of almost 40 players is no less difficult, and doubtless my final XI will give rise to much debate and inevitably disagreement. However, I have endeavoured to choose a 'typical' Arsenal side: built on a solid defence, with a strong attacking front-line, and supplied by an exceptionally talented and creative midfield. I believe the 'spine' of the team consisting of Jennings, O'Leary, Brady and Stapleton should give little cause for dissent.

1
PAT JENNINGS

The most naturally gifted goalkeeper of his era, Pat Jennings at his peak would have commanded a place in any team. His performances between the sticks for Spurs, Arsenal and N. Ireland won him a glittering array of accolades and friends the world over. He displayed in abundance the qualities of coolness, positional sense, nimbleness, alertness and bravery – qualities which set great keepers apart from good ones.

2
PAT RICE

3
SAMMY NELSON

Quite a bit of competition for the full back berths. However, I have settled for the famous N. Ireland/Arsenal partnership of the 1970s. The pair certainly proved their worth over the years, amassing almost 1,000 appearances for club and country between them. Both strong, solid defenders and capable overlappers in the best traditions of Arsenal Football Club.

4
TERRY NEILL

Strength, industry and creativity were the hallmarks of Terry Neill. Ten years of sterling service and devoted enterprise earns the former captain and manager his place in this side.

5
TERRY MANCINI

Mancini had his fair share of critics but during his brief period at Highbury, he let no one down. A solid, if unpredictable player, his wealth of experience was a major factor in David O'Leary's development as a world-class centre-half.

6
DAVID O'LEARY

A true thoroughbred and an Arsenal player through and through, David has displayed a consistency over the years second to none. Elegant, unruffled and resilient, he has been the stalwart in the Arsenal rearguard for the past 16 seasons.

7
LIAM BRADY

Recently described by Jack Charlton as the greatest Irish talent of modern times, Brady was a truly world-class player, a brilliant strategist, and possessor of probably the most renowned left foot in the game. Uncanny vision, poise, grace and silky ball skills combined to make 'Chippy' one of the game's 'all-time greats': a must for any team.

8
JOSEPH HAVERTY

A ball-playing wing wizard, 'Little Joe' was a player to brighten up any side. An entertainer of the highest order, he loved the game and the 'game' reciprocated. An ace goal-creator, he would have provided sufficient ammunition to keep any forward line busy.

9
JIMMY DUNNE

Like his partners in the strike force, Dunne was dominant in the air. He also possessed intricate close control of the ball, was always in command under pressure and, over the years, proved lethal in and around the goal area.

10
FRANK STAPLETON

Again dominant in the air, Frank was an excellent leader of the line. Ireland's all-time top striker, he possessed a good first touch for a man of his height and was totally unselfish.

11
NIALL QUINN

The big man has had his fair share of criticism in the past, but in recent years he has earned a reputation as one of the most feared strikers in the league, complementing his renowned aerial prowess with a fair smattering of delicate skills at ground level. But most important of all, Quinn has proved himself at the highest level.

TO THE FUTURE

Until recently the task of maintaining the proud tradition of the Irish at Highbury fell mainly, but not exclusively, on the shoulders of three 20-year-olds: Kwame Ampadu and centre-backs Pat Scully and Stephen Morrow. Although none of the three has ever started a league game, both Kwame and Stephen have had first team experience. During 1989–90 Kwame made two substitute appearances, and Stephen deputised for Nigel Winterburn in Arsenal's 2–1 win over Argentinian champions Independienti in Miami during the summer of 1989.

Belfast-born Stephen, a member of the Gunners' FA Youth Cup winning side in 1988, joined the club from Irish League side Bangor and was acclaimed as a rising star following his composed display in the Independienti game. However, good fortune has not smiled on the youngster since. A hernia operation coupled with an ankle injury seems to have set his career prospects back slightly. On the plus side, however, a month on loan with third division Reading, allied to a rapidly developing international career, will go a long way towards redressing the balance.

The proud owner of several Northern Ireland Youth and Under–21 caps, Stephen has already been capped at full level on three occasions and, with a contract which will keep him at Highbury until 1993, he has plenty of time in which to make a suitable impression.

Dublin-born Pat Scully, also a full international, joined the club in 1987 but failed to break into Arsenal's first team, and in March

Arsenal's chief Irish scout with two of his latest discoveries,
Kwame Ampadu and Pat Scully

1991 was sold to Southend United for £100,000. During his time as a Gunner, Scully gained valuable experience on loan to other league clubs. His first loan spell was in 1989–90 when Third Division Preston North End were the willing hosts. In September 1990 Pat jumped at the chance to link up once again with ex-Gunner Theo Foley at Northampton for a three-month stint.

Scully did not stay long at Highbury on his return from the County Ground and, in January 1991, he went out on loan again – this time to Third Division Champions Southend United, whom he joined permanently in March.

Playing regular first team football has had a tremendous impact on both Scully and Morrow. Invariably they returned from each sojourn physically and mentally stronger, sharper and oozing confidence. Consequently, the transition from reserve to first team football should not come as too much of a culture shock. Scully has already made that transition. However, he will be playing his first team football in Division Two with Southend, a fact which comes as something of a disappointment to those of us who were looking forward to yet another Irish-Arsenal defensive partnership to follow in the footsteps of Magill and McCullough, Rice and Nelson, and O'Leary and Mancini.

Another youngster who deserves mention here, and for whom a very bright future is forecast, is 18-year-old Dubliner John Bacon. John, a Youth international centre-forward, is an Arsenal trainee and is making rapid progress in the youth and reserve teams at Highbury.

In December 1990 the ranks of the Irish at Highbury were further bolstered when Arsenal signed two Irish Schoolboy internationals from Cork, striker Anthony Connolly and centre-half Roy O'Brien who joined the club in the summer of 1991. Anthony is the son of famous Cork hurler Tony Connolly, while Roy was voted Ireland's 'Young International Player of the Year' in 1989–90.

Thus, the future for the Irish at Highbury has never looked brighter, not since the halcyon days of the '70s when Arsenal boasted no fewer than seven Irish internationals in their first team.

APPENDIX 1

MAJOR IRISH SIGNINGS

Jan 1903	T. Shanks	from	Brentford	£	200
Sept 1933	J. Dunne	from	Sheffield Utd	£	8,250
Sept 1947	N. Kelly	from	Glentoran	£	650
May 1952	P. Tilley	from	Witton Albion	£	2,000
Oct 1953	W. Dickson	from	Chelsea	£15,000	
Sept 1958	W. McCullough	from	Portadown	£	5,000
May 1959	E. Magill	from	Portadown	£	5,000
Dec 1959	T. Neill	from	Bangor	£	2,500
Oct 1960	J. McClelland	from	Glenavon	£	7,000
Nov 1960	F. Clarke	from	Glenavon	£	5,000
Oct 1974	T. Mancini	from	QPR	£20,000	
Aug 1977	J. Harvey	from	Glenavon	£30,000	
Aug 1977	P. Jennings	from	Tottenham Hotspur	£50,000	

AND TRANSFERS

July 1936	J. Dunne	to	Southampton	£	2,000
March 1950	N. Kelly	to	Crystal Palace	£	8,000
Nov 1953	P. Tilley	to	Bury	£	4,000
July 1961	J. Haverty	to	Blackburn Rovers	£	17,500
Oct 1965	E. Magill	to	Brighton	£	6,000
June 1970	T. Neill	to	Hull City	£	40,000
Sept 1980	L. Brady	to	Juventus	£600,000	
Nov 1980	P. Rice	to	Watford	£	8,000
Aug 1981	F. Stapleton	to	Manchester Utd	£900,000	
Sept 1981	S. Nelson	to	Brighton	£	35,000
March 1990	N. Quinn	to	Manchester City	£700,000	
March 1991	P. Scully	to	Southend	£100,000	
May 1991	K. Ampadu	to	West Bromwich Albion	£	50,000

APPENDIX II

IRISH PLAYERS' ARSENAL CAREER RECORDS

Player	Played	Football League Apps.	Goals	F.A. Cup Apps.	Goals
Ampadu, K.	1989–91	0(2)			
Brady, L.	1973–80	227(8)	43	31(4)	2
Clarke, F.	1962–65	26		2	
Connor, M.	1902–03	14	2	2	1
Devine, J.	1978–83	86(3)		6	
Dickson, W.	1953–55	29	1	2	
Duncan, D.	1912–13	3	1	2	1
Dunne, J.	1933–36	28	10	4	3
Farrell, P.	1897–98	19	2	3	1
Gorman, P.	1982–83	5(1)			
Hannah, D.	1897–99	46	17	4	
Harvey, J.	1978–80	2(1)			
Haverty, J.	1954–61	114	25	8	1
Hill, C.	1983–84	46	1	1	
Hopkins, J.	1921–22	21	7	1	
Jennings, P.	1977–84	237		38	
Kelly, N.	1949–50	1			
Kennedy, A.	1922–27	122		7	
Mackie, A.	1922–26	108		10	1
Magill, E.	1959–65	116		11	
Mancini, T.	1974–76	52	1	8	
McClelland, J.	1961–64	46		3	
McCullough, B.	1958–66	253	4	11	
Neill, T.	1960–70	240(1)	8	12(1)	
Nelson, S.	1969–81	245(10)	10	33(2)	1
O'Flanagan, K.	1946–47	14	3	2	
O'Leary, D.	1975–	506(15)	11	64(1)	1
O'Neill, F.	1960–61	2			
Quinn, N.	1985–90	59(8)	14	8(2)	2
Ransom, F	1903–04	1			
Rice, P.	1967–80	391(6)	12	67	1
Shanks, T.	1903–04	44	28	4	1
Sloan, W.	1946–48	33	1	3	
Stapleton, F.	1975–81	223(2)	75	32	15
Tilley, P.	1953–54	1			
Toner, J.	1919–25	89	6	11	

F.L. Cup		Europe		Total	
Apps.	Goals	Apps.	Goals	Apps.	Goals
				0(2)	
23	10	13	4	294(12)	59
				28	
				16	3
8		8		108(3)	
				31	1
				5	2
				32	13
				22	3
				5(1)	
				50	17
		1		3(1)	
				122	26
4				51	1
				22	7
32		19		326	
				1	
				129	
				118	1
		4		131	
2				62	1
				49	
		4	1	268	5
15(1)	2	5		272(3)	10
27	1	19(2)		324(14)	12
				16	3
67	2	20		657(16)	14
				2	
14(2)	4			81(12)	20
				1	
36		26(1)		520(7)	13
				48	29
				36	1
26(1)	14	15	4	296(3)	108
				1	
				100	6

Substitute Appearances in Brackets

APPENDIX III

ARSENAL'S HONOUR WINNING TEAMS

Football League Division One

CHAMPIONS

1931

1930–31 Squad: Kelser, Parker, Hapgood, Jones, Roberts, John, Hulme, Jack, Lambert, James, Bastin, Johnstone, Seddon, Brain, Williams, Harper, Preedy, Male, Cope, Baker, Thompson, Haynes.

1933

1932–33 Squad: Moss, Compton, Hapgood, Male, Roberts, John, Hulme, Jack, Stockill, James, Bastin, Jones, Coleman, Haynes, Parker, Preedy, Hill, Lambert, Sidey, Cope, Parkin, Bowden, Black, Warnes, Walsh.

1934

1933–34 Squad: Moss, Male, Hapgood, Hill, Robert, John, Hulme, Jack, Coleman, James, Bastin, Birkett, Bowden, Lambert, Jones, Parkin, Sidey, DUNNE, Beasley, Dougall, Cox, Wilson, Drake, Haynes.

1935

1934–35 Squad: Moss, Male, John, Hill, Roberts, Copping, Hulme, Bowden, Drake, James, Bastin, Hapgood, Crayston, Beasley, Sidey, Marshall, Birkett, Compton, Dougall, DUNNE, Davidson, Kirchen, Wilson, Rogers, Trim.

1938

1937–38 Squad: Wilson, Male, Hapgood, Crayston, Roberts, Copping, Kirchen, Bowden, Drake, Baston, Milne, Hulme, Boulton, Compton, D. C., Compton, L. H., Biggs, Davidson, Hunt, Collett, Joy, Jones, Cartwright, Sidey, Lewis, Swindin, Griffiths, Carr, Drury, Bremner.

1948

1947–48 Squad: Swindin, Scott, Barnes, Macauley, Fields, Mercer, Roper, Logie, Lewis, Rooke, McPherson, Compton, L. H., SLOAN, Male, Jones, Wade, Compton, D. C., Forbes, Smith.

1953

1952–53 Squad: Swindin, Wade, Smith, Shaw, Daniel, Mercer, Forbes, Oakes, Goring, Lishman, Roper, Cox, Chenhall, Holton, Bowen, Milton, Logie, Platt, Kelsey, Marden, Dogin.

1971

1970–71 Squad: Wilson, RICE, McNab, Kelly, McLintock, Roberts, Armstrong, Storey, Radford, George, Graham, Marinello, Kennedy, NELSON, Simpson, Sammels.

1989

1988–89 Squad: Lukic, Dixon, Winterburn, Thomas, Bould, Adams, Rocastle, Davis, Smith, Merson, Marwood, O'LEARY, Groves, Richardson, Hayes, Caesar, QUINN.

1991

1990–91 Squad: Seaman, Dixon, Winterburn, Thomas, Hillier, Jonsson, Rocastle, Bould, Adams, Linigan, Groves, O'LEARY, Merson, Davis, Smith, Campbell, Limpar, Pates.

RUNNERS-UP

1926

1925–26 Squad: Robson, MACKIE, KENNEDY, Milne, Butler, John, Hoar, Buchan, Cock, Ramsay, TONER, Brain, Neil, Blyth, Haden, Baker, Lewis, Rutherford, J. J., Harper, Woods, Young, Rutherford, J., Lawson, Hulme, Voysey, Paterson, Parker, Seddon.

1932

1931–32 Squad: Harper, Parker, Hapgood, Jones, Roberts,

John, Hulme, Jack, Lambert, James, Bastin, Preedy, Parkin, Seddon, Hayes, Male, Moss, Cope, Williams, Thompson, Coleman, Beasley, Compton, Stockill.

1973

1972–73 Squad: Barnett, RICE, McNab, Storey, McLintock, Simpson, Armstrong, Ball, Radford, Kennedy, Graham, Roberts, George, Marinello, Blockely, Kelly, NELSON, Wilson, Batson, Hornsby, Price.

FA Challenge Cup

WINNERS

1930:

Team: Preedy, Parker, Hapgood, Baker, Seddon, John, Hulme, Jack, Lambert, James, Bastin
v Huddersfield Town (at Wembley) 2–0
Lambert, James

1936:

Team: Wilson, Male, Hapgood, Crayston, Roberts, Copping, Hulme, Bowden, Drake, James, Bastin
v Sheffield United (at Wembley) 1–0
Drake

1950:

Team: Swindin, Scott, Barnes, Forbes, Compton, L. H., Mercer, Cox, Logie, Goring, Lewis, Compton, D. C.
v Liverpool (at Wembley) 2–0
Lewis 2

1971:

Team: Wilson, RICE, McNab (Storey), McLintock, Simpson, Armstrong, Graham, Radford, Kennedy, George (Kelly)
v Liverpool (at Wembley) 2–1 (after extra time)
Kelly, George

1979:

Team: JENNINGS, RICE, NELSON, Talbot, O'LEARY, Young, BRADY, Sunderland, STAPLETON (Price), Rix (Walford)
v Manchester United (at Wembley) 3–2
Talbot, STAPLETON, Sunderland ⌄

RUNNERS-UP

1927:

Team: Lewis, Parker, KENNEDY, Baker, Butler, John, Hulme, Buchan, Brain, Blyth, Hoar
v Cardiff City (at Wembley) 0–1

1932:

Team: Moss, Parker, Hapgood, Jones, Roberts, Male, Hulme, Jack, Lambert, Bastin, John
v Newcastle United (at Wembley) 1–2
John

1952:

Team: Swindin, Barnes, Smith, Forbes, Daniel, Mercer, Cox, Logie, Holton, Lishman, Roper
v Newcastle United (at Wembley) 0–1

1972:

Team: Wilson, RICE, NELSON, Kelly, Roberts, McLintock, Armstrong, George, Radford, Kennedy, Graham (McNab)
v Leeds United (at Wembley) 0–1

1978:

Team: JENNINGS, RICE, NELSON, Price, O'LEARY, Young, BRADY, Sunderland, McDonald, Stapleton, Hudson (Rix)
v Ipswich Town (at Wembley) 0–1

1980:

Team: JENNINGS, RICE, DEVINE, Walford, O'LEARY, Young, BRADY, Sunderland, Stapleton, Hollins, Rix
v West Ham (at Wembley) 0–1

Football League Cup

WINNERS

'Littlewoods Cup'

1987:

Team: Luckic, Anderson, Sansom, Williams, O'LEARY, Adams, Rocastle, Davis, QUINN (Hayes), Nicholas, Groves, Thomas
v Liverpool (at Wembley) 2–1
Nicholas 2

1968:

Team: Wilson, Storey, McNab, McLintock, Simpson, NEILL, Radford, Gould, Graham, Sammels, Armstrong

v Leeds United (at Wembley) 0–1

1969:

Team: Wilson, Storey, McNab, McLintock, Ure, Simpson, Radford, Sammels, Court, Gould, Armstrong (Graham)

v Swindon Town (at Wembley) 1–3 after extra time

Gould

'Littlewoods Cup'

1988:

Team: Luckic, Winterburn, Sansom, Thomas, Caesar, Adams, Rocastle, Davis, Smith, Groves, Richardson (Hayes)

v Luton Town (at Wembley) 2–3

Hayes, Smith

European Competitions
European Fairs Cup

WINNERS

1970:

(1st Leg):

Team: Wilson, Storey, McNab, Kelly, McLintock, Simpson, Armstrong, Sammels, Radford, George, Graham (Kennedy)

v Anderlecht (Belgium) (Away) 1–3

Kennedy

(2nd Leg):
Team: Wilson, Storey, McNab, Kelly, McLintock, Simp-
        son, Armstrong, Sammels, Radford, George,
        Graham
        v Anderlecht (Home) 3–0 (agg. 4–3)
        Kelly, Radford, Sammels

European Cup Winners Cup

RUNNERS-UP

1980:
Team: JENNINGS, RICE, NELSON, Talbot, O'LEARY,
        Young, BRADY, Sunderland, STAPLETON, Price
        (Hollins), Rix
        v Valencia (Spain) (at Brussels) 0–0
        (agg. 4–5 on penalties)

APPENDIX IV

ARSENAL'S IRISH GOALSCORERS IN THE FOOTBALL LEAGUE: SEASON BY SEASON, 1897–98 to 1990–91

1897–98   Hannah 12; Farrell 2
1898–99   Hannah 5
1902–03   Shanks 4; Connor 2
1903–04   Shanks 24
1912–13   Duncan 1
1919–20   Toner 1
1920–21   Toner 3; Hopkins 2
1921–22   Hopkins 3; Toner 1
1922–23   Hopkins 2
1924–25   Toner 1
1933–34   Dunne 9
1935–36   Dunne 1
1946–47   O'Flanagan 3; Sloan 1
1953–54   Dickson 1
1955–56   Haverty 2
1956–57   Haverty 8
1958–59   Haverty 3
1959–60   Haverty 8
1960–61   Haverty 4; Neill 1
1962–63   McCullough 3
1963–64   McCullough 1; Neill 1
1964–65   Neill 1
1967–68   Neill 2
1968–69   Neill 2
1969–70   Rice 1; Neill 1
1971–72   Rice 1; Nelson 1
1972–73   Rice 2
1973–74   Rice 1; Brady 1; Nelson 1
1974–75   Brady 3
1975–76   Brady 5; Stapleton 4; Rice 1; Mancini 1
1976–77   Stapleton 13; Brady 5; Rice 3; Nelson 3; O'Leary 2

1977–78	Stapleton 13; Brady 9; Rice 2; O'Leary 1; Nelson 1
1978–79	Stapleton 17; Brady 13; Nelson 2; O'Leary 2; Rice 1
1979–80	Stapleton 14; Brady 7; Nelson 2; O'Leary 1
1980–81	Stapleton 14; O'Leary 1
1981–82	O'Leary 1
1982–83	O'Leary 1
1983–84	Hill 1
1985–86	Quinn 2
1986–87	Quinn 8
1987–88	Quinn 2
1988–89	Quinn 1
1989–90	O'Leary 1
1990–91	O'Leary 1

APPENDIX V

ARSENAL'S IRISH INTERNATIONALS

The following are the international career records of all Irish players who won international recognition whilst on the books of Arsenal Football Club. Many of them won further caps with other clubs but, for the purposes of this book, only the caps they won as Arsenal players are included here.

It should be noted that until 1924, there was only one Ireland team. Also, until the late 1950s N. Ireland, for the purpose of home international fixtures, were permitted to include players born in the Republic. Consequently, some players, such as Joshua Sloan, appeared for both Irish teams.

NORTHERN IRELAND (and IRELAND before 1924)

Dickson, W. (3) 1953 v England; 1954 v Wales, England.

Jennings, P. A. (42) 1977 v Iceland, Holland, Belgium; 1978 v Republic of Ireland, Denmark; 1979 v Bulgaria (twice), England (three times), Scotland, Wales, Denmark, Republic of Ireland; 1980 v Israel; 1981 v Scotland (three times), Portugal, Sweden, Israel; 1982 v England, Wales, Yugoslavia, Honduras, Spain, France; 1983 v Albania, Scotland (twice), England, Wales, Austria, Turkey, West Germany; 1984 v Wales, Finland (twice), Romania; 1985 v England, Spain, Turkey.

Kennedy, A. L. (2) 1923 v Wales; 1924 v England.

McClelland, J. (5) 1960 v West Germany; 1961 v Wales, Italy, Greece, West Germany.

McCullough, W. J. (9) 1961 v Italy; 1963 v Spain (twice), Scotland, England; 1964 v Wales, Uruguay, England, Switzerland.

Mackie, J. A. (1) 1923 v Wales.

Magill, E. J. (21) 1961 v Scotland, Greece, England; 1962 v Poland (twice), England, Scotland; 1963 v Wales, Spain (twice), Scotland, England; 1964 v Wales, Uruguay, England, Switzerland (twice), Scotland; 1965 v Holland, Albania, Scotland.

Morrow, S. (2) 1990 v Uruguay (sub), Poland.

Neill, W. J. T. (44) 1961 v Italy, Greece (twice), West Germany, Scotland, England; 1962 v Wales, England, Poland; 1963 v Wales, Spain (twice), Scotland, England; 1964 v Wales, Uruguay, England, Switzerland, Scotland; 1965 v Holland (twice), Wales, Albania (twice), Scotland, England; 1966 v Wales, West Germany, Mexico, Scotland; 1967 v Wales, Scotland, England; 1968 v Israel, Turkey (twice); 1969 v England (twice), Scotland (twice), Wales (twice), USSR (twice).

Nelson, S. (48) 1970 v England (sub), Wales, Spain; 1971 v Cyprus, England, Scotland, Wales, USSR (twice); 1972 v Spain, Scotland, England, Wales; 1973 v Bulgaria, Cyprus, Portugal; 1974 v Scotland, England, Sweden; 1975 v Yugoslavia, Sweden, Norway; 1976 v Israel, England, Belgium (sub); 1977 v West Germany, Wales, Iceland (twice), Holland, Belgium; 1978 v Wales (sub), Republic of Ireland, Denmark; 1979 v Bulgaria (twice), England (three times), Scotland, Wales, Denmark, Republic of Ireland; 1980 v Israel; 1981 v Scotland (twice), Portugal, Sweden.

Rice, P. J. (49) 1968 v Israel; 1969 v USSR; 1971 v England, Scotland, Wales, USSR; 1972 v Spain, Scotland, England, Wales; 1973 v Bulgaria (twice), Cyprus, England, Scotland, Wales, Portugal; 1974 v Scotland, England, Wales, Norway; 1975 v Yugoslavia (twice), England, Wales, Scotland, Sweden, Norway; 1976 v Israel, Scotland, England, Wales, Holland, Belgium; 1977 v West Germany, England, Scotland, Iceland (twice), Holland, Belgium; 1978 v Republic of Ireland, Denmark; 1979 v England (three times), Scotland, Wales, Denmark.

157

Shanks, T. (2) 1903 v Scotland; 1904 v Wales.

Sloan, J. W. (1) 1947 v Wales.

Toner, J. (6) 1922 v Wales; 1923 v Wales, England; 1924 v Wales, England; 1925 v Scotland.

REPUBLIC OF IRELAND

Brady, W. L. (26) 1974 v USSR, Turkey; 1975 v Switzerland (twice), USSR, Turkey; 1976 v Norway, Poland, England, Turkey, France; 1977 v France, Spain, Bulgaria (twice); 1978 v Norway, Northern Ireland, England; 1979 v Denmark, Bulgaria (twice), West Germany, Argentina, Wales; 1980 v England, Cyprus.

Devine, J. A. (7) 1979 v Czechoslovakia, Northern Ireland; 1981 v Czechoslovakia, Holland; 1982 v Algeria, Spain; 1983 v Malta.

Dunne, J. (3) 1936 v Switzerland, Hungary, Luxembourg.

Haverty, J. (15) 1956 v Holland, Denmark, West Germany; 1957 v Denmark, England (twice); 1958 v Poland (twice), Austria; 1959 v Sweden; 1960 v Chile, Wales, Norway; 1961 v Scotland (twice).

Mancini, T. J. (1) 1974 v USSR.

O'Flanagan, K. P. (3) 1946 v England; 1947 v Spain, Portugal.

O'Leary, D. A. (55) 1976 v England, France; 1977 v France, Spain, Bulgaria (twice); 1978 v Norway, Denmark, England; 1979 v Bulgaria (twice), West Germany, Argentina, Wales, Northern Ireland; 1980 v England, Cyprus, Holland; 1981 v Czechoslovakia, Poland, Holland, France; 1982 v Holland, Iceland; 1983 v Spain; 1984 v Poland, Israel, China, USSR, Norway, Denmark; 1985 v Israel, England (sub), Norway, Spain, Switzerland (twice), USSR, Denmark; 1986 v Wales; 1988 v Spain, 1989 v Malta (twice),

Hungary, West Germany, Northern Ireland (sub); 1990 v Wales (sub), USSR, Finland, Romania (sub), Turkey, England (twice), Poland, Chile.

Quinn, N. J. (13) 1986 v Iceland (sub), Czechoslovakia; 1987 v Bulgaria (2 sub), Luxembourg (sub), Israel; 1988 v Romania (sub), Poland (sub), Norway (sub), England (sub), Tunisia (sub), Spain (sub); 1989 v Hungary (sub).

Scully, P. J. (1) 1988 v Tunisia (sub).

Sloan, J. W. (2) 1946 v Portugal, Spain.

Stapleton, F. A. (24) 1976 v Turkey, France; 1977 v Spain, Bulgaria (twice); 1978 v Norway, Denmark, Northern Ireland, England (sub); 1979 v Denmark, West Germany, Argentina, Wales, Bulgaria, Northern Ireland; 1980 v England, Cyprus (twice), Holland, Belgium, France; 1981 v Belgium, Czechoslovakia, Poland.

NORTHERN IRELAND 'B'

McCullough, W. J. (1) 1959 v France.

REPUBLIC OF IRELAND 'B'

Scully, P. J. (1) 1990 v England.

UNDER–23

NORTHERN IRELAND

Clarke, F. R. G. (4) 1962, 1963, 1964, 1965 v Wales.

Magill, E. J. (1) 1962 v Wales.

Morrow, S. (1) 1990 v Republic of Ireland.

Neill, W. J. T. (4) 1962, 1963, 1964, 1965 v Wales.

Nelson, S. (1) 1969 v Italy.

Rice, P. J. (2) 1968 v Wales; 1969 v Italy.

REPUBLIC OF IRELAND

Scully, P. (1) 1990 v Northern Ireland

UNDER–21

REPUBLIC OF IRELAND

Ampadu, K. (2) 1990 v Malta, Turkey.

Scully, P. J. (4) 1989 v England; 1990 v Malta, Turkey, England*.
* While on loan to Northampton

NORTHERN IRELAND

Hinnigan, J. (1) 1990 v Israel.

YOUTH INTERNATIONALS

REPUBLIC OF IRELAND
K. Ampadu, W. L. Brady, J. A. Devine, R. Duffy, P. A. Gorman,
P. J. Scully, F. A. Stapleton.
NORTHERN IRELAND
A. J. Hinnigan, S. Morrow.